Children's Dreams in Clinical Practice

Children's Dreams in Clinical Practice

Stephen Catalano, D.S.W.

Plenum Press • New York and London

Library of Congress Cataloging-in-Publication Data

Catalano, Stephen.
    Children's dreams in clinical practice / Stephen Catalano.
        p.   cm.
    Includes bibliographical references.
    ISBN 0-306-43308-7
    1. Child psychopathology. 2. Child psychology. 3. Children's
dreams.   I. Title.
RJ499.C299 1990
154.6'34'083--dc20   89-28470
                                                                  CIP

© 1990 Plenum Press, New York
A Division of Plenum Publishing Corporation
233 Spring Street, New York, N.Y. 10013

Printed in the United States of America

This book is dedicated to Margaret,
for her love and encouragement throughout this project;
to family and friends for their support;
and to the purple lion and the pink frog,
who prove that sometimes dreams really do come true.

Preface

Once upon a time I dreamed myself a butterfly, floating
like petals in the air, happy to be doing as I pleased, no
longer aware of myself! But soon enough I awoke and then,
frantically clutching myself, Chuang Tzu I was! I wonder:
Was Chuang Tzu dreaming himself the butterfly, or was
the butterfly dreaming itself Chuang Tzu?

—Chuang Tzu

Dreams are an endless source of mystery and fascination.
Those we remember bring to our conscious awareness
a variety of characters, circumstances, and situations
often implausible or even bizarre in our everyday world.
Sometimes dreams are more mundane and common-
place, reflecting memories of recent events of obvious
importance.

It is perhaps because of our lack of ability to understand fully the origin of dreams or interpret their exact

meaning that dreams are the subject of such interest and speculation. Or perhaps, as the Chinese philosopher Chuang Tzu suggested, they allow us the freedom to expand our thoughts, associations, or spirit in a way that no other experience, waking or otherwise, can.

Clinical interest in dream content has primarily been limited to the psychoanalytical perspective. This modern clinical interest in dreams is the direct result of Freud's landmark contribution concerning the importance of dreams in unconscious thought and in the practice of psychoanalysis. Theoretically, psychoanalytical interpretation of dream content as a repressive–defensive content function dominated clinical practice and application for many years and remains an influential school of thought.

Recent theoretical contributions have focused on more adaptive properties and highlighted a developmental perspective. In this way the meaning and use of dream content in clinical practice also have evolved into a broader application. As a result of technological and methodological advances in data collection, much more is now known about the dreams of children and adults. The data collected have enabled dream content to be examined from a variety of perspectives and provided a much broader diagnostic and therapeutic application in clinical practice.

After an extended dormant period in which the use of dream content was restricted to psychoanalytical applications, an exciting rapprochement has occurred, utilizing the developmental and adaptive properties of dreams. This book is an attempt to explain for the reader the contemporary theory and use of dream content in clinical practice and its application with children and adolescents.

Stephen Catalano

Gilford, New Hampshire

Contents

Part I. Introduction 1

Chapter 1. Why Study Children's Dreams? 3

*Chapter 2. The Significance and Use of Dream Content
in Clinical Practice with Children and
Adolescents* 7

Part II. Dream Content: Theory and Research 17

Chapter 3. Theoretical and Historical Review 19

The Meaning of Dream Content 20
The Meaning of Children's Dreams 23
Dream Content of Emotionally Disturbed Children 28

Chapter 4. Methodological Issues in the Study of Dream
        Content   31

Confabulation   33
Manifest versus Latent Content of Dreams   37

Chapter 5. Children's Dream Content as an Indicator of
        Developmental Functioning   41

Review of Developmental Theory   41
Research on Dream Content as an Indicator of
        Developmental Functioning   45

Part III. The Study   53

Chapter 6. Introduction and Background   55

Review   55
Design and Methodology   57
Hypotheses Tested   57
Population and Samples   57

Chapter 7. Procedures   61

Interview Procedure   61
Tests Conducted   62
Instruments   63
    Structured Recall   63
    Elkan Checklist   65
    Rating the Dream   66
    Other Instruments   68
Validity and Reliability   68

Chapter 8. Findings and Analysis   73

Hypothesis I   73
    Quantitative Analysis   73

Qualitative Analysis 82
Hypothesis II 87
    Quantitative Analysis 87
    Qualitative Analysis 93
Summary 97

Part IV. Theoretical Implications and Practice
    Techniques 103

Chapter 9. Contributions to Dream-Content Theory 105

Differences in the Dream Content of Emotionally
    Disturbed Adolescents 106
The Association between Developmental
    Function and Dream Content 107
The Use of Clinical Practice as the Laboratory
    Setting 110
Review and Suggestions for Further Study 111

Chapter 10. Clinical Applications and Techniques for
    Use in Practice 117

Enhancing Dream Recall 117
School-Aged Children.......................... 122
Adolescents.................................... 131
Contraindications and Other Clinical Uses 135

Part V. Normal and Emotionally Disturbed Children's
    Dream Content 141

Chapter 11. The Latency-Aged Child 143

Chapter 12. Dreams of Adolescents................. 147

Chapter 13. Dreams of Children with Specific
Problems 153

Sexually Abused Children 153
Medically Ill Children 155
Children of Divorce 157

Part VI. Helping Parents Understand Their Children's
Dreams 159

Chapter 14. Introduction for Parents 163

Chapter 15. What Are Dreams? 169

Learning about Sleep 169
Dreaming 171
When Do Dreams Begin? 172
Distinguishing Dreams from Fantasy and
Daydreams 173

Chapter 16. What Do Dreams Mean? 175

What Children's Dreams Mean 176
Developmental Issues 177
Different Dreams at Different Ages 179
Dreams of the Preschooler 179
Dreams of the Early School-Aged Child 180

Chapter 17. What about Nightmares? 183

What Do Nightmares Mean? 184
Why Do Children Have Nightmares? 185
Night Terrors 187

Chapter 18. Techniques for Parents.................. 189

Techniques to Improve Dream Recall 190
Communicating about Dreams 193

Appendixes 197

Appendix A. Erikson's Eight Stages of
    Psychosocial Development 197
Appendix B. Dream Scores Derived from the Elkan
    Checklist by Age 198
Appendix C. Mack's Dream Scores of Normal
    and Disturbed 14–15-Year-Old Boys 198
Appendix D. Categories of Disturbed Adolescents
    Used in This Study 199
Appendix E. Cover Letter for Treatment Providers 201
Appendix F. Consent Letter for Parents 203
Appendix G. Consent Form 204
Appendix H. Data Analysis Design 205
Appendix I. Definition of Terms 209

References 211

Index 219

Part I

Introduction

Chapter 1

Why Study Children's Dreams?

Dreams have been a source of interest to human beings from the beginning of time. There have been a variety of theories and much speculation about dreams and their meaning. The meaning of dream content has been misunderstood often, seldom studied, and generally underutilized in clinical practice. Because of their often unusual quality and content, children's dreams are of particular interest to parents, professionals, and children themselves.

There has been, however, relatively little empirical research on the study of children's dream content and even less on the effects of emotional disturbances upon dream content. Much of the available data has been derived from research conducted throughout the past 20 years. Of particular interest is the burgeoning school of thought that suggests dream content of children is less representative of repressed instictual drives and wishes as was once believed and more indicative of psychosocial development (Elkan, 1969; Foulkes, 1982; Mack, 1974). Results of more recent research concluded that children's dream content reflects a developmental continuum similar to waking behavior, and children with emotional disorders reported dream content different from that of children without such disorders. These conclusions indicated a need for further study of the dream content of children and adolescents.

This book has two primary objectives. The first is to provide the reader with a contemporary conceptual framework for understanding the dream content of children and adolescents. The second objective is to identify and describe differences in the dream content of those children and adolescents with emotional disturbances from those free from such disturbances. In doing so, it is the principal aim of this book to demonstrate the usefulness of dream content theory when applied in clinical practice.

If an accepted theoretical approach to understanding childhood development, such as the Eriksonian psychosocial stages, can be associated with the dream reports of children, such a connection would be of tremendous value to clinical practice. An association between a theoretical orientation and dream content would enhance the existing means for understanding the behavior of children and adolescents as well as the emotional disturbances that affect them. A child or adolescent who is experiencing conflict with a particular developmental stage may recur dream content reflective of that developmental stage. Regardless of the nature, degree, or type of conflict, or whether or not the conflict is seen as a temporary regression or a fixation, the dream content may be reflective of the dreamer's level of developmental functioning.

In addition to these important theoretical implica- tions, there are a number of applications and considera- tions vital to clinical practice. Besides the usual diagnostic and assessment techniques available to practitioners, dream reports can be utilized to help determine the level of de- velopmental functioning or dysfunction. Important events, memories, and experiences assist in establishing another means of therapeutic communication with a child or an adolescent. The diagnostic and treatment uses of dreams for clinical practice with children and adolescents are considerable.

Chapter 2

The Significance and Use of Dream Content in Clinical Practice with Children and Adolescents

Two of the major developments in clinical practice with children and adolescents have occurred within the past 35 years:

- The shift of emphasis from instinct theory to adaptation theory and coping stemming from ego-psychology theory
- The advent of child-development theory, which has been a major resource for understanding the process of normal childhood and emotional problems

Important contributions have been made to the theoretical and clinical understanding of development and psychic structure. Many investigators (Erikson, 1959; Hartmann, 1950; Hartmann & Lowenstein, 1945, 1946, 1949; Jacobson, 1964; Kernberg, 1975, 1980; Kohut, 1971,

1974, 1977; Kris, 1950; Lewis, 1973; Mahler, Pine, & Bergman, 1975; Winnicott, 1965) have added significantly to such research. These authors concluded that psychological development is based upon successful progression through each sequential stage of development; any unresolved conflicts result in a fixation or delay that impedes the process of subsequent psychological development. The child who is regressed or fixated at a specific level of developmental functioning may manifest behaviors indicative of some unresolved conflict associated with that stage of development. The earlier the disruption, the more severe the disturbance. Of particular relevance to understanding this point of view is Erikson's (1959) epigenetic principle of growth and behavior elaborated upon in Part II of this book.

In child psychoanalysis, the use of children's dreams has been discussed frequently (Bornstein, 1946; Winget & Kramer, 1979; Rangell, 1956) and at times intensely debated (Freud, 1946; Klein, 1932). Despite differences, there appeared to be little debate about the importance of dreams in understanding children. Throughout this century, the usefulness of dreams in child analysis and psychotherapy has been suggested by many theorists (Ablon & Mack, 1980; Fraiberg, 1965; Freud, 1927; Palombo, 1978).

Despite advances in developmental theory, including recent research suggesting that children's dream content is reflective of developmental functioning, little empirical research has been conducted to link these two aspects in clinical practice. Utilization of recent data on the dream content of children is potentially significant for any clinician who works with children or adolescents. Understanding the dream content of emotionally disturbed children and adolescents and how it is different from that of "normal" children is of tremendous importance. If dream reports of emotionally disturbed children and adolescents reflect a significant difference in the developmental functioning expected at that specific age, dream-content reports become an important additional diagnostic and therapeutic technique in clinical practice.

The diagnostic assessment of a child is achieved through a variety of means. Symptomatology, social behavior, play observation, previous history, family history, and therapeutic interaction are utilized in determining the developmental level and psychosocial functioning of a child. The dream content of a child or adolescent may serve as another indicator of the developmental level of the child. Dream-content reports may also serve as an ongoing means of assessing conflicts and growth throughout the therapeutic process. For example, in one study recall was enhanced when children were asked to remember and report dream content. That process increased the child's introspective skills. The child's associations to the dream report, subsequent verbal response, and play are all valuable mechanisms available to the clinician for understanding the meaning of dream content (Green, 1971).

Although the importance of dream material in clinical work with children is of diagnostic and therapeutic value, the utilization of dreams in practice is problematic. This relates primarily to theoretical and methodological issues concerning younger children's dream content and its use in clinical practice.

Much has been written about the methods of revealing the unconscious in child psychotherapy and the use of dreams in that process. Anna Freud (1965) wrote about the use of the transference relationship in treating children in psychotherapy and the important role of dream content in understanding the unconscious content of a child's thoughts. Klein (1932) maintained a different perspective: she believed that play, drawing, fantasies, and dream content can be substituted for verbal association and may reveal a child's unconscious thought content.

As a child's underlying psychological dynamics become known to the therapist, the latent meaning of dreams becomes apparent and can provide a concise, pointed reflection of that child's conflicts, ego structure, and developmental issues. As with dream material of an adult patient, the therapist profits most by knowing the child's association to the dream. Children can be asked their associations to a dream without causing any unusual degree of anxiety or disturbance. In that respect, dream material may function like play, fantasy, or drawing. Through derivative figures, stories, or characters, important thoughts are addressed without the anxiety that conscious awareness can bring. Dream content is indicative of the developmental conflicts of the child and serves as a diagnostic measure of the child's ego functioning, defensive style, and coping ability (Catalano, 1984).

Having witnessed the benefits derived from applying dream-content theory, we believe that dream material is underutilized in all clinical work, not just that involving children. The majority of clinicians are unfamiliar with the process, content, and meaning of dreams and their use in clinical practice. This may be the result, in part, of the weighty psychoanalytical influence that cautioned against dream use or interpretation unless the therapist was trained as an analyst. Psychoanalytical theory implies that dreams are an important element in understanding the unconscious thoughts of a patient. Yet, the highly symbolic quality of psychoanalytical interpretation, and the absence of clinically relevant empirical data pertaining both to the processes of sleep and dreaming and to the meaning of dream content of children discourage its use in nonpsychoanalytical practice.

Dreams reported in psychoanalysis were an important source for building psychoanalytical theory. Freud's contributions as a theorist, however, overshadowed the empirical limitations of his data base. According to Foulkes (1982), Freud's biased sample of patients in psychoanalysis and the use of his clients' spontaneous and selective recall of their dreams produced a distorted sample of all dream content. Experience suggests that most clinicians are unfamiliar with knowledge gained over recent years regarding the process of dreaming and the meaning of dream content. The uncertainty of clinicians regarding such issues as when children begin to dream, their ability to distinguish dreaming from fantasy, and the meaning of dream content serves to inhibit the use of dream content in clinical practice with children and adolescents.

Without knowledge of the meaning of children's dream content, the clinician's interest and ability to solicit dream content from clients and use it in a productive way are necessarily diminished. The therapist may also feel uncomfortable dealing with the material. As a result, a clinician may choose not to respond to or explore a dream reported by a client. This also serves to inhibit further dream disclosure by the child, who may feel that dreams are unimportant or not of interest to the therapist. Thus, a valuable method of determining the child's level of functioning at the point of assessment or during the treatment process itself has gone unused. Likewise, an important tool in establishing a therapeutic relationship as an additional means of communicating about a problem between the child and the therapist is neglected. The following illustrations of dream content are offered in support of this point of view.

The content of children's dreams often represent unconscious conflicts and difficulties in the ego functioning of a child. One nine-year-old with a presenting problem of oppositional behavior and anger at home reported a dream during his seventh treatment session:

> Carl stated that he had a dream last night during which somebody had come into his house and poisoned his whole family except him. He didn't know who did it or why, but after that, he went to live with Mr. T. (of television and movie fame). Carl and Mr. T. then cleared woods with bulldozers and built strong log homes nobody could get into, and they lived there together.

Carl was a boy who had recently been displaced as the "man" of the family by a new stepfather and two older (by five and seven years) stepbrothers. Prior to that change, he had been a main source of support to his somewhat depressed and dependent mother and was the "protector" for his twin brother who suffered from a seizure disorder. The dream was indicative of his anger at the changes in the family composition and was particularly aimed at his stepfather, whose involvement had disrupted an intense attachment Carl had to his mother. His anger was manifested by the death—from an unknown source—of his family, perhaps indicative of his primitive rage as well as oedipal fears of his stepfather, who cooked the family meals. Carl then moved in with a T.V. character—a personification of masculine identity for many boys and a prominent figure in their culture at the time the dream was reported. Together they engaged in rugged activity and built a fortress. Carl and Mr. T. were then invulnerable to any threat or interference, symbolically reflective of the fears, anxieties, and conflicts that

Carl was subject to at home as a result of his mother's recent remarriage.

Developmentally, Carl, who was nine at the time the dream was reported, would be expected to be functioning within Erikson's fourth stage of psychological development: identity versus inferiority. This stage, which corresponds to the latency stage of development (ages five or six to eleven or twelve), is associated with the primary task of learning about the world. It is at this stage of development that the child acquires and is most concerned with skills and knowledge that enhance self-identity and self-esteem. Carl's dream, however, reflects violent and physically agressive themes, in which threats and danger are paramount. Carl must protect and isolate himself in his dream against the dangers of the outside world. These themes are more reflective of Erikson's third stage of development: initiative versus guilt, which parallels Freud's phallic or oedipal period (approximately ages three to five). Carl's dream, in a number of ways, reflects the delayed level of developmental functioning that he exhibited in his waking life. His dream, then, can be utilized to corroborate his delayed developmental conflicts and to further indicate the nature and degree of these conflicts: namely, his unresolved overattachment to his mother and the associated anger, rage, and fear he experiences towards his stepfather. Furthermore, the dream report can be used as a vehicle to address the conflicts therapeutically. Carl was asked what he thought of the dream. His responses quickly led to his thoughts on his family, particularly his stepfather. Carl discussed how his stepfather's cooking tasted like "poison" and how he preferred his mother's cooking. From this advantage, we quickly were able to discuss his feelings of displacement and rejection in reaction to his mother's remarriage.

A 16-year-old adolescent, seen for an evaluation relating to her placement in a group-home, revealed the
following recurring dream:

> Sarah dreamt of her parents being upset with her for
> some unknown misbehavior. She then recalled her
> mother coming into the bathroom, removing her from
> the toilet, and begin punishing (i.e., slapping) her.
> She recalled being very young (preschool age) at this
> time and added she was not allowed to pull up her
> clothing and was immediately put to bed.

For Sarah, recent placement had triggered a great deal
of stress, and her dream reflected many of her central
concerns. The history of parental abuse, both physical and
sexual, was directly revealed in the discipline methods
used by her parents in the dream. These events occurred
during her bathroom movements in a state of undress,
reflecting the sexual abuse she was subject to as well as
her concern regarding her mother's sexuality. The inability to clothe herself reflected her powerlessness and victimization. Being taken to her bedroom was indicative of
Sarah's placement away from home. Developmentally, the
recurring dream signals primitive fears of harm from primary love objects as well as issues of control and conflicted sexuality. Sarah's world was threatening, dangerous, and unpredictable. Control issues were evident and
may have mirrored behavioral problems as well as the
acting out of expressions of anger.

Recurring dreams like the one above provide an added
significance in that they are reflective of more significant themes, issues, or conflicts for the dreamer. The
recurring quality suggests that they are indicative of central dilemmas or issues. Such dreams serve as self-dis-
closing reflections of self-identity—who and what we feel

we are—and reveal any consistent concerns or conflicts experienced.

Many adults and some adolescents will report recurring themes of falling or running. Frequently, the dreamer is hampered or handicapped in his or her efforts to run or escape from a frightening or threatening object, figure, or person. Often the dreamer reports being tied up or bound while trying to run or unable to use his or her feet to run or escape. More traditional psychoanalytic theory and symbolism suggests that these typical recurring themes indicate a generalized or specific dilemma or conflict for the dreamer. The effort to escape the conflict or threat is reflective of the dreamer's anxieties regarding the ability to deal effectively with the conflicts he or she faces.

Younger children experience or report fewer recurring dreams than adolescents or adults. The reasons for this are unclear. Perhaps consistent conflicts or self-identity themes have not had adequate time to develop in children. Assuming that identity formation and related issues are not likely to manifest until adolescence, recall ability perhaps may be a contributing factor and will be addressed further in subsequent chapters.

Interpretations of the dream material made at the appropriate time in therapy, like other verbal and nonverbal interventions, facilitate an understanding of the child's conflicts and ego functioning. It also may facilitate a mutual communication process between the child and the clinician, thereby leading to an understanding of confusing or unusual thoughts. The process of verbalizing dreams may also enhance ego functioning by supporting the child's capacity to put his fantasies into words and to think about them with the therapist. Thus, the dream reports of children and adolescents serve a multitude of diagnostic and therapeutic functions and purposes.

Part II

Dream Content: Theory and Research

Chapter 3

Theoretical and Historical Review

Interest in dreams has existed in all cultures throughout time. Primitive cultures believed the dream may have been a communication from the Gods. Van de Castle (1971) reviewed dream theories from various ancient cultures and reported that, during the Age of Reason in the eighteenth and nineteenth centuries, dream research fell into scientific disrepute as a result of its subjectivity. It was not legitimized until Freud (1900) theorized that dreams were a vehicle for penetrating the hidden core (or unconscious) of the personality. Winget and Kramer (1979) reported that investigators from various disciplines increasingly became interested in the dream as a type of personal document, like a diary or autobiography. They also cited that numerous sociologists and anthropologists used the dream to gain knowledge about the relationship between the individual and society. To these investigators, the dreams reported by a society's members served as metaphors depicting the relationship of these people to their society.

THE MEANING OF DREAM CONTENT

Freud's *The Interpretation of Dreams* (1900) was, according to Brenner (1974), as revolutionary and monumental a contribution to psychology as *The Origin of Species* was to biology 50 years earlier. Freud wrote the following in the third (revised) English edition, published in 1932: "It (dreaming) contains, even according to my present day judgment, the most valuable of all discoveries it has been my good fortune to make. Insight such as this falls to one's lot but once in a life time" (17, p. xxxii). Green (1971) has elaborated upon the significance of this work to various fields of therapy and noted that Freud himself considered this piece of writing to be so important that he revised and amplified his book of dreams on eight separate occasions.

Freud first became aware of the significance of dreams in therapy when he realized that his patients frequently described their dreams in the process of free association. He believed that the conscious experience during sleep, which the dreamer may or may not recall after waking, was the manifest content of the dream. Freud referred to the unconscious thoughts and wishes that threaten to wake the sleeper as the latent content of the dream. Finally, he labeled the conscious mental operations of transforming the latent content into the manifest content as the dream work. Freud concluded that dreams, like neurotic symptoms, were the conscious expression of unconscious fantasies or wishes not readily accessible in waking life.

In *The Interpretation of Dreams* (1900), Freud theorized about dreams as being reflective of the unconscious thoughts of the mind. In that work, he used his famous dictum regarding symbolism of dreams: "The interpretation of dreams is the royal road to the unconscious activities of the mind" (Freud, 1900, p. 647). He believed that dreaming was a primitive kind of thinking (primary process) in which instinctive wishes were represented as being at least partially fulfilled. Freud originally considered children's dreams pure wish fulfillment: clear, coherent, easy to understand, and unambiguous in their style. He subsequently revised that view, when, in his *Introductory Letters of Psychoanalysis* (1916) he wrote: "You must not suppose, however, that all children's dreams are of this kind (wish fulfillment)" (p. 117). Freud believed that "dream distortion sets in very early in childhood and dreams (dreamt by children) between five and eight have been reported which bear all the characteristics of latter (adult) ones" (Freud, 1916, p. 117).

He also believed that dreams served a defensive–repressive function for instinctual drives, particularly in the process of transforming latent dream material into manifest content. He thought that children's dreams represented a direct, undisguised fulfillment of a wish, and that the fulfillment of the wish was the content of the dream. Freud proposed that the distorted, defensive quality of dreams first appeared after the ages of four or five. Many of these views are still held by psychoanalytical theorists and practitioners today, but they comprise a small minority view in the current study of children's dreams.

Others have proposed various meanings regarding dream content and its relationship to waking personality and experience. Two of Freud's early associates, Adler and Jung, proposed dream theories totally contrasting each other in their relationship to the dream experience and waking behavior. Adler (1931) suggested dreams were essentially continuous and consistent with one's waking behavior. Jung (1974) on the other hand believed that the "style of life" one developed in dreams served as "complementary" or compensatory functions, and that dreams brought out those aspects of the total self that did not find expression in waking life. Current research findings (Foulkes, 1970; Trupin, 1976) generally support the theory of waking dream continuity as conceptualized by Adler. Hartmann (1964) agreed with Freud's theory of dreaming but added that, similar to repetitive play, dreams enable the child to master traumatic experiences.

Recent theory on dream content has focused on the adaptive work of the ego and on the problem-solving aspects of dreams. There has been an increasing interest in the ego functions and the developmental psychology of dream content, particularly the dream content of children. French and Fromm (1964), Greenberg and Pearlman (1975, 1978), and Jones (1970) have written about the adaptive aspects of dreaming. Monchaux (1978) suggested not only that dreams help one structure internal and external experiences, but that communicating dreams help the dreamer master these experiences: dreams may reinforce the functioning of the ego. Hirschberg (1966) also described the importance of verbalization in ego development and wrote about the ego development required to describe dreams.

Palombo (1978) combined the traditional psychoanalytic view of dreams and the more recent information-processing models. He described the autonomous mechanism of nonconscious adaptive ego functioning called the memory cycle when he wrote:

> The memory cycle is a sequence of processes through which
> new experimental information is introduced into adap-
> tively suitable locations in the permanent memory struc-
> ture. The most striking hypothesis of the memory cycle
> model is that the critical step in the sequences—the step
> which matches representations of closely related experi-
> ences of the past—takes place during dreaming. (p. 13)

Rather than contrasting with the psychoanalytical
emphases on wish fulfillment—drive discharge and cen-
sorship—the adaptive aspects of dreams are complementary and approach the formation and function of dreams
from different perspectives. Others (Foulkes, Larson,
Swanson, & Rardin, 1969; Foulkes, Pivik, Steadman, Spear,
& Symonds, 1967; Green, 1971; Markowitz, Steadman,
Spear, & Symonds, 1963; Markowitz, Borkert, Sleser, &
Taylor, 1967) have written about the influence of important dimensions of everyday life that may influence the
manifest content of dreams: cultural, familial, and social
elements. Ablon and Mack (1980) have described how developmental stress such as toilet training, oedipal conflicts, the birth of a sibling, changes in home or school,
and other such traumas will find their way into the manifest content of children's dreams. According to these authors, dreaming serves an adaptive and mastery function
for the dreamer regarding these issues.

THE MEANING OF CHILDREN'S DREAMS

The work of Freud and psychoanalytical theory influenced the early research on children's dreams. Some of
the early studies of children's dreams focused on the
identification of content in children's dreams, considered
to be a means for understanding the unconscious thought

processes (Blanchard, 1926; Cason, 1935; Foster & Anderson, 1936; Jesild, 1933; Selling, 1932; Witty & Kopel, 1971). Early researchers attempted to classify various dream content derived from the verbal material of the dreams themselves. Because these studies varied in the age range of subjects, there was a lack of consistency in their findings. While all of the studies mentioned that differences in dream content occurred as a function of age, none agreed as to the nature of these differences. Freud's emphasis on the latent content of dreams resulted in the subsequent neglect of and resistance to the study of manifest dream content. The lack of consensus was due in large part to the absence of a theoretical model to apply to these findings. The concept of a continuous developmental process was not available at that time, and researchers were able to do little more than note the distinction in dream content of children of various ages.

A critical development in the scientific study of dreams occurred in 1953 with the observation of rapid eye movement (REM) sleep (Aserinsky & Kleitman, 1953), which triggered new directions in the research on dreams and the dream process. However, the majority of early research involved adults. In an extensive review of dream research, Winget and Kramer (1979) reported that out of the 132 studies involving dream content analysis, only 13 references were found to children's dreams; only three of these dealt with the dreams of emotionally disturbed children or adolescents.

The research of Foulkes and his associates (1967) was the first to utilize the EEG in a laboratory setting with children. From these studies evolved a major school of thought and a method of studying dream content. Foulkes (1967) examined the dreams of 32 boys, ages 6–12 years. From the manifest content of these dreams, collected under laboratory conditions and scored blindly by judges, Foulkes concluded that the REM dream content of normal children was realistic in characterization, setting, and plot; it was relatively free of bizarre symbolism and unpleasant affect.

Subsequent studies by Foulkes *et al.* (1969) found the same qualities in the dreams reported by younger children (ages 3–4) of both sexes and older boys (ages 13–15). Generally, these dreams were described as realistic and related to everyday life. Parents, siblings, and peers tended to be characters in dreams that involved play, social interaction, and achievement.

Based on his longitudinal studies, Foulkes' (1982) findings challenged theories about the psychoanalytical content of children's dreams as reflective of disguised infantile wishes and impulses. Foulkes believed children's dreams stereotypically followed a developmental continuum dictated and constrained by general waking ability corresponding to the chronological age of the child. His interpretive framework was that of the dream as an ego process that was continuous rather than discontinuous with waking ego functioning. Thus, the major focus of dream-content research was the concern arising from the interaction with environmental, personal, and social demands relative to one's chronological and developmental level of functioning.

Another researcher, Hall (1953, 1966), portrayed dreams as cognitive–symbolic processes capable of revealing how people think of themselves in relation to significant others and the world in general. Foulkes (1982) believed his own data were a striking affirmation of Hall's thesis, and indicated the potential of dream study for revealing what and how children think of themselves.

Hirschberg (1966) described how verbalizing dreams

served a significant function in ego development. He explained how the process of looking at and seeing dreams can help define and delineate the limits of reality. He also found that dreams reflected conscious and unconscious conflicts (wishes, powerful affects, reality) in which a child struggled to organize and cope with unpleasant dimensions of life. In a similar vein, Foulkes (1969) described adaptive ego functioning present in dreams. He studied the effect of external stimuli during sleep as demonstrated by the externalization and displacement of the disturbing stimulus in the subjects' dreams.

Elkan (1969) demonstrated that the manifest content of children's dreams reflected the developmental concerns appropriate to age as delineated by Erikson's (1959) psychosocial theory of development. Elkan hypothesized that the dreams of children of different ages reflected developmental differences as identified in Erikson's developmental model. Specifically, she believed that the concerns central to each developmental level would appear at the time designated by Erikson's model and not before, consistent with the epigenetic principle upon which Erikson's theory was based. Elkan's hypothesis was proven. Her study was the first systematic attempt to study children's dreams within a theoretical framework based on developmental psychology. Elkan's work was the first to confirm the hypothesis that a relationship existed between manifest dream content and the developmental level of functioning.

Recent theorists and researchers of dreams have written about the adaptive, problem-solving aspects of dreams. Ablon and Mack (1980) state: "From this perspective, the manifest content of dreams, rather than being seen as a vehicle for important latent thoughts, reflects a person's attempts to cope with emotionally important

material of that day or the days just preceding the dream"
(p. 172). Dreaming seemed to help structure internal and
external experiences. A processing-like system appeared
to occur in typical dreams, whereas only selected issues
made their way into consciousness.

After nearly a century of evolution in theoretical approaches to and research on dream content, a rapprochement between the traditional psychoanalytic model of wish
fulfillment and the more adaptive ego-functioning model
has resulted. Such a rapprochement incorporates the pro-
cess-like coping mechanisms evident in the dream material of children, as well as acknowledging the developmental continuum, its associated tasks and conflicts, and
the presence of instinctual drives and wish fulfillment.

The use of dream-content material in clinical practice
is no longer limited to the psychoanalytical perspective of
representations of wish fulfillment and instinctual drives
alone. The results of the research and theory throughout
the past 30 years have produced a broader perspective for
conceptualizing and understanding children's dreams and
the meaning and use of their content. These changes have
incorporated some of the views of child-development
theory and ego psychology that address the timely progression of age specific issues and emphasize the adaptive quality of emotional development. The effects have
produced a demystification of dream content. The highly
symbolic, sophisticated psychoanalytical imagery had been
of use only to those who had that theoretical orientation
and specialized training. The adaptive and developmental model for understanding children's dream content in-
creases the theoretical and practical applications of dream
content in clinical practice with children and adolescents;
such a model has become an integral part of the procedure of the therapist in working with children.

DREAM CONTENT OF EMOTIONALLY
DISTURBED CHILDREN

Psychoanalytical theories have shaped the interpretation of the meaning of dreams experienced by emotionally disturbed children. Initially, Freud suggested that dream content demonstrated instinctual drives and wish fulfillment. Later, Anna Freud (1965) emphasized that children's dreams reflected a repertoire of defensive mechanisms. Her focus on children's dreams emphasized latent content and psychoanalytically derived symbolism used to interpret the dreams of children and adolescents in treatment.

The research of Foulkes was the first extensive research collected on the dreams of children and adolescents. Foulkes (1969) began to report on the dream content of children and adolescents with emotional disturbances, which he thought was "generally realistically related to waking life and . . . became relatively more bizarre and unpleasant for children with some dysfunction in waking personality" (p. 641).

Foulkes' conclusions were derived from studies (Foulkes & Rechtschaffen, 1964) of the dream content of young adult males whose "vivid fantasy" in dreams were associated with personality pathology; the dreams of these subjects were associated positively with pathological scales on the Minnesota Multiphasic Personality Inventory (MMPI). Latency-age boys whose dreams had been rated most bizarre were judged to be least competent in dealing with everyday life (Foulkes & Pivik, 1969). Foulkes (1969) also conducted a comparison study of the dreams of emotionally disturbed adolescents with those of a control group; this study found that the dreams of the controls had greater freedom from psychological distress and were more conventional than those of the emotionally disturbed group.

In another study, Langs (1967) compared the dreams of emotionally disturbed adolescents with those of adults who had similar pathology. He reported that the dream content of the adolescents was developmentally different from that of the adults. He suggested that developmental differences existing between the groups were responsible for this discrepancy.

Mack (1974) conducted a study to investigate developmental differences reflected in the manifest content of normal and disturbed children's dreams. She compared groups of emotionally disturbed and "normal" 8–9-year-olds and 14–15-year-olds using Erikson's model of psychosocial development as the theoretical framework for determining their developmental levels. Mack concluded that the dream content of the disturbed adolescents was significantly lower developmentally than that of normal adolescents. While unable to statistically confirm similar conclusions from the dream content of the emotionally disturbed 8–9-year-olds, she reported a significantly higher proportion of developmental conflict for the experimental group than for the controls. Mack's research was particularly significant because of two important factors. First, she confirmed Elkan's (1969) theory of different developmental levels reflected in the dream content of children of different ages. Second, she confirmed the developmental differences in the dream content of the emotionally disturbed adolescents when compared with the dream content of "normal" adolescents.

Chapter 4

Methodological Issues in the Study of Dream Content

Research on the study of dream content is surprisingly limited in the number of empirical studies conducted since the turn of the century. Winget and Kramer (1979) compiled an impressive collection of data, reviewing the content and methodology employed in every dream content study available to that date. Possible reasons for the lack of research on dreams may be related to the extraordinary influence of psychoanalytical thought upon dream theory as well as to certain methodological difficulties in the collection and study of dream content.

Freud's (1900) early writings on dream content as a reflection of wish fulfillment resulted in a dominance of psychoanalytical theory in the work with dream content. In succeeding years, knowledge and clinical use of dream content were obtained, for the most part, from adults in psychoanalysis or psychotherapy. The dream reports, so important to the development of theoretical constructs, were often collected from small and highly biased samples of those involved in psychoanalysis or psychotherapy (Foulkes, 1982). Such spontaneously recalled dreams have proven to be an unrepresentative sample of total dream content. Weisz and Foulkes (1970) reported that, because of the affective component involved in frightening, conflicted, or traumatic-like dreams, an inflated number is spontaneously recalled, and the actual content of dream material for adults and children is more notable for its mundane and tranquil themes than was once believed.

As noted, one of the most important developments in the scientific study of dreams and dream content occurred in 1953 with the observation of rapid eye movement (REM) sleep (Aserinsky & Kleinman, 1953) and its correlation with dreaming stages. The possibility of investigating the dream closer to its occurrence and in relation to a number of physiological processes stimulated the extensive use of laboratories in the study of dreams. More recently, with the recognition that mental content could be recovered from all the electroencephalographically defined stages of sleep, interest in the concurrent process of the non-REM portion of sleep has developed (Foulkes, 1962, 1969; Pivik & Foulkes, 1968). Foulkes (1982) reported that recent work by experimentally oriented researchers began to stress the cognitive–skill component of adult dreaming. Such research may produce valuable insights into mental operations, memory processing, and other cognitive operations. Others such as Hobson and McCarley (1984) focused their attention on physiological processes. They theorized about the neurotransmitter shift of norepinephrine and serotinin in the pons region of the brainstem, which may account for shifts from waking to sleeping during dreams.

Studies of sleep and dreams have been undertaken by various disciplines, and sleep and dreams continue to be studied from cognitive, physiological, and psychological perspectives. A number of limitations in the methodology of the study of dreams and dream content exist, however. The latter will be examined more fully in the following section.

CONFABULATION

Two key issues concerning the validity of children's dream-content studies exist. The first involves the accuracy of the dream report, and the second concerns what methods are used to determine the meaning of dream content.

When do children begin dreaming and how do we know when a child is actually reporting a dream? Is the report of a dream some form of selective memory of important events, fantasy, or mere fabrication?

Fraiberg (1959) and Lewis (1973) believed that children begin dreaming in their first year of life. Sleep research studies have indicated that infants spend an unusually high proportion of their sleep in REM sleep: up to 80% of the total sleep for premature infants. Observations of sleeping infants' behavior suggest that certain distress—as evidenced by crying, moaning, and motoric movements—is not caused by physiological needs such as hunger or discomfort, but is suggestive of some internal source. This stress is often relieved by some comforting reassurance such as a gentle pat on the back by a caring parent or adult.

As language develops throughout the second year, confirmation of the child's capacity to dream becomes possible, but questions about the child's ability to distinguish a dream from reality are raised. The child's capacity to differentiate dreams from waking fantasy, daydreams, imaginative play or real events is influenced by a number of factors. Language development, intelligence, and expressive ability are influential in the process of correctly identifying dreams.

Piaget (1929) described three stages in children's understanding of dreams. In the first stage, occurring at ages 5–6, the child experiences the dream as coming from outside. In the second stage, ages 7–8, the dream begins to take on some internal qualities as to its source. The dream itself, however, remains external—within the room or in front of the child's head. In the third stage, at ages 9–10, the child generally experiences a dream as internal—as part of him- or herself. In reality, there are questions about the content of the subject's dream. What in essence is studied is the dream report of the dreamer, not the actual dream. This subject has frequently been debated by dream researchers. Masserman (1944) notes:

> No dream as such has ever been analyzed—or ever will be analyzed—until we develop a technique of reproducing the dream sequence itself on a television screen while the patient is asleep. All we can do at present is to note carefully the patient's *verbal and other behavior patterns* while he is talking "about" his hypothetical "dream" during some later analytic hour, remembering all the while that his hypogogic imagery has inevitably been repressed and distorted in recollection, that it is described in words and symbols colored by his experiences not only before but since the "dream" and that in the very process of verbalization his "descriptions" and "associations" are further dependent

on his unconscious motivations in telling the dream at all,
his transference situation, his current "ego defenses," his
physiologic status and the many other complex and inter-
penetrating factors of the moment. (p. 6)

Foulkes (1982) referred to the work of Rechtschaffen,
(1967) who contended that confabulation constituted no
general impediment to meaningful research on dreams.
The criticism that dream studies did not measure dreams
at all but only the waking cognitive process of memory
and verbal description has been demonstrated to be highly
implausible. Through sleep laboratory experiments using
violent films, Foulkes (1982) found that dream reporting
of children was not related significantly to differences in
waking stimuli. His results confirmed that cognitive processes of memory and verbalization alone were not responsible for differences in dream content. Foulkes' findings supported the conclusions of Winget and Kramer
(1979) when they stated: "Again, with some indirect evidence we assume a significant correspondence between
the dream as reported despite there having been a double
shift from visual and sleeping while experienced to verbal
and waking when reported" (p. 13) (Bussell, Dement, &
Pivik, 1972; Roffwarg, Dement, Muzio, & Fisher, 1962;
Vaughn, 1964).

Foulkes (1982) further addressed the question of the
validity of dream content when he wrote at the conclu-
sion of his longitudinal studies:

It is *not* true that spontaneous fantasy cannot be studied
following rigorously empirical methods. We can make
meaningful observations of dream differences in dreamers'
knowledge basis and neuro-cognitive abilities. We can
search for the story grammars that characterize dream narratives. We can study reliably and systematically the as-

sociative contexts to which these elements have been re-
cruited for dream representation. (p. 277)

Without the ability to record the dream as it happened, efforts were made to reduce the time between the
occurrence of the dream and the dream report. For example, it was presumed that to awaken the EEG-moni-
tored sleeper during REM stages of sleep and collect the
dream report reduced the distortion, regression, and confabulation potential.

A conflict exists among therapists and researchers regarding the reliability of dream-content studies that depend upon so-called nonrepresentative samples (i.e.,
dreams collected from spontaneous recall or from a clinical population). Theorists who have written extensively
about children's dream content from clinical populations,
such as Ablon and Mack (1980), have defended this approach. They suggested that reliable data can be generated, which can provide a further understanding of clinical issues, child development, and the process of dream
content. They cited the quality and depth of the interpersonal relationship between dreamer and the interviewer,
which was not the same within a laboratory setting. They
also noted the increased understanding of latent content,
which helped provide meaning to the manifest dream
content.

Confabulation has never been empirically tested, but
rather only impressionistically addressed by dream researchers. While a commitment to the scientific process
must be strictly adopted in clinical work and all other behavioral sciences, a rigid adherence to limited and nar-
row research paradigms that prevent or discourage research of this kind is not warranted. There is a need to
empirically study more representative samples of children's dreams. No scientific field can attribute impor-

tance to any subject with only speculative and impressionistic data. The dream content of children needs to be studied in the laboratory as well as in the clinical setting.

While limitations and methodological problems exist in both areas, efforts to integrate the work of the laboratory with that of the practice arena must continue. Such continued collaborative efforts of theory building and empirical research will further enhance the usefulness of both in clinical work, thus enabling the clinical practice field to better understand and utilize dreams in diagnosis and treatment.

MANIFEST VERSUS LATENT CONTENT OF DREAMS

Freud's (1900) original assumption—that the meaning of children's dreams is simpler and less disguised than that of adults—resulted in research that addressed only the manifest content of dreams, the assumption being that manifest content and latent content were the same. While some theorists, researchers, and clinicians (Blanchard, 1926; Freud, 1965; Klein, 1932) began to doubt the value of manifest dream content as an indicator of unconscious thought, the research that followed in the 1930s began to focus on the differences in the manifest content of dreams versus that of the latent content (Cason, 1935; Foster & Anderson, 1936; Jersild, Markey, & Jersild, 1933; Selling, 1932; Witty & Kopel, 1971).

Elkan (1969) reported that the growing interest and development of ego psychology and its focus on defense and coping mechanisms may have directed the interest of clinicians to latent content for clues to the "dream work" as opposed to "dream thought," which Freud (1953) believed to be the "essence of dreaming" (p. 506). He contended that the interpretation of the latent content of the dream with a perspective to the dreamer's unconscious drives was the key to the meaning of the dream. The interest in adaptation increased the attention received by the manifest content as psychologically significant in understanding dream content. Some theorists and clinicians continued to stress the critical elements of the latent content of dreams in children: "If the meaning of dreams is to be explored in relation to its latent content, the central life dilemmas of the individual may be found to be economically expressed" (Ablon & Mack, 1980, p. 197). Others suggested that the latent content of dreams is a step away from the original dream material and produces what can be referred to as an association to associations: "As the centrifugal force of the process of free association propels the latent material further from the dream, the links to the original stimulus become more and more tenuous, and the interpretation of meaning necessarily relies more on inference" (Elkan, 1969, p. 22).

Elkan noted Freud's (1959) case of Dora, with the progression from "jewelry case" to "jewel drops" to "drops" to "wetness" to "bedwetting" and "sexual wetness" as an example of intricate reconstruction of associations leading back to the "meaning of the dream." She cautioned against the reliance on inferences necessary to make the conceptual leap from "jewelry case" to "sexual wetness." She also questioned the validity of the inferred meanings.

According to Elkan, reliability of judgments about data becomes questionable, perhaps more reflective of the clinician's skills rather than the function of the dream. Erikson (1954) suggested that clinicians may pay lip service to the analysis of the latent meaning in dream content and cautioned against viewing the manifest meaning as merely superficial. He used projective techniques as an example, which he stated "have shown that any segment of overt behavior, reflects as it were, 'the whole store' " (p. 138). On the basis of his research, Erikson suggested the need for the development of adequate techniques to carefully assess the meaning of manifest content (Erikson, 1954). Elkan (1969) reported two studies (Reiss, 1951; Sheppard & Karon, 1964) designed to test Erikson's hypothesis that results based on manifest dream content alone will correlate with results based on the manifest plus latent content. The results of both studies were positive, supporting the view that much can be learned about the meaning of dreams from the manifest content.

Chapter 5

Children's Dream Content as an Indicator of Developmental Functioning

REVIEW OF DEVELOPMENTAL THEORY

The past 35 years have produced a change in emphasis in psychodynamic theory, which has influenced the clinical field. Developmental theory, which focuses on the processes of progressive growth and development throughout the life cycle, has enriched and supplemented instinct and drive theory with its emphasis on psychopathology.

Developmental theory is psychosocial in orientation and is progressive and sequential in nature. Any developmental stage incorporates those intrapsychic and social tasks most important to the child at that particular stage of growth. Successful completion or mastery of any stage of development is usually considered necessary to ensure continued growth and maturation in a subsequent stage. As Lewis (1973), who has written about the developmental influences upon clinical practice, describes:

> . . . development is a complex process. There is a constant order of succession from one stage to another. Each successive stage in normal development represents an advance from the previous stage. (p. 11)

The theory of intrapsychic development is important in understanding the significance of children's dream content as an indicator of developmental functioning in clinical work with children. Intrapsychic structure encompasses the differentiation of self-representation and object representation and their related ego defense mechanisms. Ego-psychology theory and object-relations theory regarding the development of intrapsychic structure have a history that can be traced to Freud's introduction of structural theory in 1923. Anna Freud *(The Ego and the Mechanisms of Defense,* 1966) expanded the understanding of the defensive structure of the ego and introduced the modern day conceptualization of defense mechanisms. Hartman (1939, 1964) introduced several propositions, particularly the focus on the process of adaptation that formed the backbone of modern psychology. He also collaborated with Kris (1945, 1954) and Loewenstein (1946, 1949) on a series of papers that delineated the nature of formation of psychic structure, aggression, and superego formation.

More recent theory builders (Blanck & Blanck, 1979; Kernberg, 1980; Mahler, 1963, 1968; Mahler, Pine, & Bergan, 1975; Stern, 1985; White, 1974) have contributed to the understanding of the ego and its psychosocial development. Intrapsychic structure develops through the slow, progressive differentiation of the self-representation from object representation and the parallel and related maturation of defense mechanisms (Jacobson, 1964b; Kernberg, 1976; Kohut, 1971, 1977; Mahler, 1968; Masterson, 1981). In their work, Mahler *et al.* (1975) concluded that the developmental process consists of three progressive stages:

- Autistic
- Symbiotic
- Separation–individuation

Mahler identified four subphases of the separation–individuation stage: differentiation, practicing, rapprochement, and on the way to objective constancy. A failure to master a stage along this developmental continuum, according to Mahler, resulted in some difficulty in the process of the formation of both self-representation and object representation, as well as in difficulties in related ego functions associated with specific subphases of separation–individuation.

Wherever a lesion, fixation, or conflict in development occurs, corresponding manifestations of ego pathology will occur. If the arrest occurs in the symbiotic phase, self-representation and object representation become fused. The person then employs psychotic ego defenses such as denial, poor reality testing, and disturbed ego boundaries. If the arrest or fixation occurs in the rapprochement subphase of separation–individuation, self-representation and object representation become separate and split into polarized good and bad self-representation and object representation characteristic of borderline personality organization. If the arrest occurs on the way to object constancy, self-representation and object representation are at an integrated stage—whole rather than split. The successful completion of the separation–individuation stage allows for the emergence of an oedipal level of development with increasingly mature ego defenses such as intellectualization, sublimation, isolation, and reaction formation. It is with entry into this stage of development that neurotic organization or conflict can characterize psychological distress.

Erikson (1959) described human development as following an "epigenetic principle" that states that anything that grows has a "ground plan." From that ground plan, parts arise, each part having its time of "special ascendency" until all parts have risen to form a functioning whole (1959, p. 52). Erikson postulated eight stages of psychosocial development, each centered around special developmental tasks, focal crises, and conflicts generated by changes experienced within the growing individual. Active mastery of each stage is essential to the continuing development of a healthy personality. Failure to adequately cope at any one stage leaves the individual vulnerable to the conflicts of that particular stage. The theory also suggested probable impairment in resolving successive stages.

Erikson's psychosocial developmental theory supplements or complements the psychoanalytical view of psychosexual stages of development. According to Rappaport (1959), Erikson's unique contribution to the concepts of ego psychology was to expand Hartmann's adaptation theory by extending the developmental schedule from birth to old age within a psychosocial content. Erikson also specified the nature of social encounters and the implications of success or failure at each level of development. Erikson's eight stages or crisis levels of development are listed in Appendix A.

The meaning of children's dream content needs to be analyzed and understood within the context of developmental theory. Dreams reflect developmental functioning and help the child in mastering the tasks and conflicts associated with each stage of development. Dreaming assists the child in adapting to the changes that occur through each consecutive stage of growth and development. Dream content also reveals the unresolved developmental tasks from previous stages which the child may be struggling to master or contain.

RESEARCH ON DREAM CONTENT AS AN INDICATOR OF DEVELOPMENTAL FUNCTIONING

The research and theory most germane to this study are associated with child-development theory. As Winget and Kramer (1979) noted:

> . . . large gaps remain in the information available about changes in dream content across the entire life cycle. The data that will be gathered about dream content across the life cycle will have to be examined in concept with some theoretical system which delineates the phases of the life cycle, such as Erikson's, if a maximal contribution to our knowledge of the possible role of the dream is to be obtained. (p. 24)

Of particular interest is the work of those who have attempted to identify the level of developmental functioning indicated in the dream content of normal and emotionally disturbed children. Elkan (1969) was a pioneer in studying the dream content of children vis-a-vis their developmental level of functioning; she used Erikson's psychosocial theory of development. Elkan hypothesized that the dreams of children of different ages would reflect the epigenetic developmental model. Theorizing that the psychosocial crises central to each developmental level would appear at the time designated in Erikson's model and not before, Elkan predicted that her subject's dream content would reflect the level of developmental functioning appropriate or corresponding to his or her age.

Her subjects were 66 white, upper-class males from a resort community outside New York City. The sample included 20 boys 4–5 years of age; 26 from 8–9 years of age; and 20 from 14–15 years of age. Each age group was selected to fall within the age range for a particular developmental level as delineated by Erikson:

- 4–5   years: Stage III, Initiative versus Guilt
- 8–9   years: Stage IV, Industry versus Inferiority
- 14–15 years: Stage V, Identity versus Role Diffusion

Using a checklist based on Erikson's descriptions of the conflicts of each developmental stage, judges scored the dreams for the presence of characteristics related to various developmental stages.

Elkan's hypothesis was confirmed (Appendix B demonstrates the distribution of developmental levels indicated in the dream content for each of the three groups). Her research was the first to confirm a relationship between the manifest content of dreams and developmental functioning.

As noted earlier, very little research has been conducted on the dreams of emotionally disturbed children. Foulkes *et al.* (1969) conducted a comparison study of the dreams of seven 13–15-year-old working-class boys living in an institution for emotionally disturbed adolescents; he compared them with control subjects of the same age living in the same community. Foulkes hypothesized that the dreams of the experimental group would show a positive correlation of dream vividness and affect with the presence of those subjects' pathology. Following two nonconsecutive nights in a sleep laboratory, each subject was given the Wechsler Intelligence Scale for Children (WISC) and California Psychological Inventory. The results of the latter test indicated that the controls had greater freedom from psychological distress and were more conforming and conventional than the experimental group.

Dream ratings supported Foulkes' hypothesis. Disturbed adolescents' dreams were rated more imaginative, less related to everyday expe rience, more unpleasant, and more physically aggressive than those of the control group. When compared to a previous study (Foulkes, 1967) of 6–12-year-olds, the normal adolescent's dreams increased in work and study themes in comparison to the latency-age group in the previous study. The dreams of the institutionalized adolescent boys increased in the category of "diffusely organized gravel or movement dreams (e.g., riding around in a car)."

The latter finding was of particular interest because of the implications for developmental differences between the two groups. In Erikson's theory, adolescents of this age (13–16) are early in the fifth stage of psychosocial development (identity vs. role diffusion). Issues of the role of work or study in regard to a career are of paramount concern. Foulkes' normal subjects reflected these issues in their dreams, while the emotionally disturbed adolescents struggled with issues less mature or developmentally below what would be expected for their age group. Foulkes concluded that dreams "are generally realistically related to waking life and . . . become relatively more bizarre and unpleasant for children with some dysfunction in waking personality" (Foulkes & Pivik, 1969, p. 641).

In another investigation focused on the presence of developmental differences in dream content, Langs (1967) examined fifteen 11–17-year-olds who were in outpatient treatment for emotional problems and compared them with fifteen adults, 20–49-years-old, of similar psychopathology. The diagnosis of each group included schizophrenic reaction, borderline personality disorder, severe neurosis, and character disorders. The subjects' dreams were coded, randomized, and scored blindly by two raters as to the appearance of unconscious conflicts. Although Langs did not state what criteria his raters used to determine the presence, absence, or quality of dream characteristics, he reported that the raters' reliability ranged from 70% to 100%.

The results confirmed Langs' hypothesis that the adolescents' dream content was characterized by qualities associated with that stage of development which differed developmentally from those of the adults. Langs described the dreams of the disturbed adolescents as containing more "phallic destructive representations," few modified aggressive derivatives, more self-concern, narcissism, and more reality impairment than those of the disturbed adults (pp. 43–52). These results were consistent with the psychoanalytical framework for understanding adolescence, which included concerns with body images, narcissism, and grandeur associated with the withdrawal of cathexis from parents. Although Langs did not report careful methodological details of his research, his results were consistent with the hypothesis that developmental differences are reflected in the dreams of emotionally disturbed adolescents and adults.

Mack (1974) conducted a study of 70 white, working-class and lower-middle-class to middle-class boys in Westchester County, New York, to determine the developmental differences in the dream content of emotionally disturbed and normal children. Thirty-five of the subjects were 8–9 years of age; the remaining 35 were 14–15 years of age. The 8–9-year-olds corresponded to Erikson's stage four of psychosocial development: industry versus inferiority; the 14–15-year-olds corresponded to the fifth stage of development: identity versus role diffusion.

Within the 8–9-year-old subjects, 18 boys were identified as normal and 17 were identified as disturbed. The criteria utilized by Mack for the "normal" boys included positive social and emotional adjustment, academic performance congruent with school expectations, and no present or past referral for psychotherapy treatment. The "disturbed" children were identified by their involvement in a class for emotionally disturbed children and present activity or past referral for psychotherapeutic treatment (see Mack, 1974, for additional criteria).

The developmental level of each dream was determined through the use of the Elkan (1969) checklist, which is theoretically based on Erikson's developmental theory. Mack also incorporated four scales from Hall's (1966) classification system for content analysis of dreams. This is a system that quantifies the manifest content of the verbal report by covering all of the major characteristics of the dream content such as setting, characters, activities, success or failure, and aggression.

Each subject's dream was rated according to Elkan's (1969) developmental checklist. The checklist was designed to score each dream report in a manner consistent with Erikson's epigenetic model; each subject's developmental level was determined by the highest level scored on the checklist. As previously noted, Erikson viewed development as a continuous process in which the organism evolves through successive stages of growth, each characterized by its own central crises. The child's developmental stage was defined by the latest level of achievement attained. Following a period of training, two judges rated each of the 144 items on the checklist in relation to each of the 70 dreams; the judges agreed on 90% of the items.

Mack's hypothesis that the developmental level of the disturbed adolescent was significantly lower than the normal adolescent's was confirmed (see Appendix C); comparisons between the two 14–15-year-old groups were significant (at the .05 level using a one-tail test). The hypothesis was not supported with respect to comparison between the two 8–9-year-old groups. However, a significantly higher proportion of developmental conflicts with the disturbed 8–9-year-old group was found. Despite the lack of statistical corroboration in the developmental level of the two 8–9-year-old groups, the disturbed group's dreams revealed notably greater difficulty with a major issue of their developmental stage: castration anxiety. It was found that the dreams of the disturbed 8–9-year-olds scored relevantly higher on this scale.

The reasons for these results were not clarified. The lack of significant difference may have been related to the developmental levels of the participants, which were lower than expected. They may also have been related to the low socio-economic status of the participants.

The impact of these results upon clinical practice with children may be crucial. Dream material reported in psychotherapy sessions can be utilized with an increasing degree of confidence as an indicator of the child's level of developmental functioning, and it is therefore a good diagnostic tool. The implications for the diagnostic and treatment process with children are of significance, especially in evaluating the child's behavior and developmental functioning. These results provide a link between the dream content of children and adolescents on the one hand and developmental and ego-psychology theory on the other. Children and adolescents with emotional disturbances will reflect different (i.e., lower) developmental functioning in their dream content than those adolescents and children without emotional disturbances.

In our study, we tested Mack's (1974) hypothesis that developmental differences in the dream content of emotionally disturbed and normal adolescents (ages 14–16) would differ significantly and, secondly, examined the effects of specific emotional disturbances upon the dream content of those adolescents with emotional difficulties. Some methodological changes were made to improve the reliability and validity of the study. The test of the second hypothesis was an original study; it was an attempt to contribute to knowledge about the dream content of various categories of emotionally disturbed adolescents and to study its implications and use for clinical practice.

Part III

The Study

Chapter 6

Introduction and Background

REVIEW

This research was conducted to test two hypotheses. The first hypothesis tested was that a difference exists in the developmental level reflected in the dream content of "normal" adolescents on the one hand and emotionally disturbed adolescents on the other. The second hypothesis tested was that adolescents with more severe emotional disturbances will reflect a greater delay or more immature level of developmental functioning in their dream content than those with less severe emotional disturbances. Only adolescents were used in the study because of the greater reliability in dream recall they provide.

Elkan (1969) first established that children's dream content reflected developmental functioning; Mack (1974) reaffirmed this position with her results and established that developmental differences exist in the dreams of "normal" and emotionally disturbed adolescents. Our research was conducted, in part, to retest the same hypothesis that developmental differences do exist between "normal" and emotionally disturbed adolescents.

Positive results in this study further support a relationship between dream content and developmental theory. A correlation between adolescents with emotional disturbances and delayed developmental functioning in dream content would be established if the first hypothesis is supported.

The second hypothesis was based on this predicted association between dream content and developmental theory. This hypothesis predicted that, much like normal developmental processes and ego impairment, a corresponding continuum of developmental functioning will be reflected in the dream content of the disturbed adolescents. It is assumed that the dream content of "normal" adolescents is indicative of their expected developmental level. The hypothesis suggested that among a group of emotionally disturbed adolescents, those whose diagnosis is indicative of a more primitive, immature, or delayed developmental level will reflect a corresponding primitive or immature developmental level in their dream content. Consistent with that hypothesis, those whose disturbances are theoretically indicative of a developmental level below what is expected of the normal group but more mature and developed than those with more primitive or immature delays should likewise reflect the corresponding developmental levels or differences in their dream content.

DESIGN AND METHODOLOGY

The independent variable was the two populations of adolescents to be studied: Population 1 (Ued) was the group of adolescents with emotional disorders and Population 2 (Un) was the group of "normal" adolescents. The dependent variable was the developmental level reflected in the dream content of each subject.

Each respondent's dream was rated at the level of developmental functioning reflected in the manifest dream content. The instrument used (Elkan's checklist) produces a measure of developmental functioning reflected in the dream content to correspond with Erikson's eight stages of psychosocial development.

HYPOTHESES TESTED

The manifest dream content of the emotionally disturbed group of adolescents will reflect differences in developmental functioning from the dream content of adolescents without emotional disturbances.

Those adolescents with more severe emotional disturbances will reflect a greater developmental delay or a more immature level of development functioning in their dream content than those with moderate emotional disturbances; the latter will reflect a greater developmental delay than those with mild emotional disturbances.

POPULATION AND SAMPLES

Data were collected on the dream content of 54 adolescents (N = 54) between the ages of 14 and 16 years. The subjects were selected randomly from schools, clinics, hospitals, and private practices in a mixed rural, urban, and resort areas in central New England. The communities were heterogeneous in socio-economic composition and included a mixture of professionals from various occupations and backgrounds, as well as a number of blue-collar and working-class families. The population was almost entirely white and of mixed political and religious affiliations. The ethnic background of the population was primarily multi-generational French-Canadian and Anglo-Saxon with a small scattering of various other ethnic groups. The sample size was determined using a power of analysis calculation and research conducted by Mack (1974) for determining a statistically significant population size.

Subjects included both males and females. The sample was comprised of two groups, each with 27 subjects. An experimental Group A (N = 27) was selected randomly from the cases of various mental health centers, child and family services agencies, and private practitioners in the geographic area. Two residential treatment facilities were used to collect dreams from seriously disturbed adolescents who were not likely to be found in outpatient treatment. The emotionally disturbed group was comprised of subjects who were in psychotherapy and suffered from an emotional disturbance that met criteria for a diagnosis under the American Psychiatric Association's *Diagnostic and Statistical Manual of Mental Disorders,* Third Edition (DSM-III) (1980).

Independent raters (a child and youth clinician and the researcher) reviewed a list of problems and symptoms each subject presented; they rated each subject in the emotionally disturbed group by their level of emotional disturbance:

- Group AI   (Ed-se) Severe emotional distur-
                   bances such as psychotic and af-
                   fective disturbances
- Group AII   (Ed-mo) Moderate emotional dis-
                   turbances such as anxiety disor-
                   ders and identity or mood distur-
                   bances
- Group AIII   (Ed-mi) Mild emotional distur-
                   bances such as adjustment disor-
                   ders or phase of life stress reac-
                   tions

(See Appendix D for a complete description of the symptoms associated with each category.)

An interrater reliability score of 89% was achieved
between the raters, which ensured accuracy and reliability of classifications within the emotionally disturbed
groups. A low percentage of agreement would have
threatened the validity of the theory that dream content
reflected different levels of developmental disturbances.

The group of adolescents without emotional disturbances was selected from various schools within the same
geographic area. These subjects were asked to participate
based upon the following criteria: positive social and academic functioning as determined by their teachers; no
known past or present emotional disturbance requiring
psychotherapy. While operationally difficult to ensure
"normalcy," the criteria eliminated all but perhaps the most
mildly disturbed subjects, rendering them indistinguish-
able from the rest of the control group.

Chapter 7

Procedures

INTERVIEW PROCEDURE

In order to facilitate the participation of children with emotional disorders, a letter (see Appendix E) describing the research was sent to the appropriate directors and administrators of clinics and treatment facilities in the region. That letter was followed by phone contact requesting participation of their staff. Private practitioners were contacted in a similar fashion. If their response was positive, further inquiries were made requesting that the therapist explore the interest of their adolescent patients in the study. A brief description of the study was given to the patient and his or her parents, and then the researcher contacted the parents by letter (see Appendix F) to introduce himself. The purpose and intent of the study was stated as "an effort to learn more about children's dreams"; permission for the child to participate was requested. If permission was granted, the child was asked if he or she would meet with the researcher to discuss participation in a study about his or her dreams. A written consent specifying the nature of the study and the adolescent's role in it was signed at that time (see Appendix G).

The children in the nontreatment group (Group B) were selected from public middle and senior high schools in the area. The appropriate school administrator was personally contacted, the study was explained, and a request to approach teachers and parents was made. Similar procedures were used with teachers and parents to explain the study and to request consent for the adolescents to participate. The researcher then spoke to those students interested in participating in order to explain the purpose of the study and the procedure for collecting the dream reports. Written consent was obtained at that time.

TESTS CONDUCTED

A *t* test for two independent samples was conducted between group A and B in order to differentiate: 1. the developmental level reflected in the dream content of the emotionally disturbed adolescents and 2. the developmental level reflected in the dream content of the "normal" adolescents.

The *t* test was used to determine whether the criterion means for the two groups differed significantly. The unit of measure was the developmental level of each child and the criterion or dependent variable used was the developmental level reflected in the dream content of both groups of adolescents. The Elkan checklist was the instrument for determining the developmental level of the dream content and was used as an instrument for establishing a dependent variable.

A one-way analysis of variance was used to test the hypothesis that those children with more severe emotional disturbances will reflect developmental levels in their dream content different from those without emotional problems. Appendix H provides a detailed design of the data analysis.

INSTRUMENTS

Structured Recall

Many methodological variables exist in the study of dreams and the measurement of dream content. Although drawings have been used, verbal reports for dream measurement is employed most frequently (Winget & Kramer, 1979). We have noted that such protocols vary significantly from ones that include everything a subject reports to rigorously defined coding systems that are highly selective of content.

Spontaneous recall methods have been criticized as too loose and unrepresentative of dream content (Foulkes, 1982). Regimented laboratory monitoring and awakenings have been the subject of criticism because of the artificial setting and the lack of interpersonal exchange (Ablon & Mack, 1980).

Nonlaboratory settings can be used as an efficient means of data collection as well as a therapeutic environment in which clinical work with children can take place. While valuable for their precision and representative data collection, however, laboratory settings are extremely expensive, time consuming, and impractical for clinical research. In order to promote their utilization, methodological approaches to data collection for practitioners must be easy to use, compatible with the therapeutic process, and beneficial to the client. The structured recall format has been found to be a useful and valuable tool for this purpose.

Structured recall includes an introduction to dreams and the method of data collection a day before the dreams are collected. Each respondent is asked to have paper and pen or pencil near his or her bed at night. They are then asked to write (and/or draw) anything that can be remembered about dreams they had that night as soon as they awaken the next morning. The children are further instructed that they need not *have* a dream to participate, but can write about a dream they recently had if they don't remember any from the previous night, or they can "make up" a story or dream. They are asked to identify the latter, which are later excluded from the study. These methods guard against confabulation by allowing the subject to participate even if he or she does not have a dream. The next day the children are interviewed individually and asked to describe their dreams to the interviewer who asks them to "tell [me] what you remember about your dream(s) last night, using [your] own notes or drawing(s) to assist [you]."

The researcher then follows the procedure below to elicit the dream material:

1. The subject is asked to describe everything he or she can remember about his or her dream.
2. When the respondent is finished, the researcher asks the subject to elaborate on the outcome, the

characters involved, the dream feelings, motives, mood, and the setting with the researcher inquiring about such details by asking "then what happened after that?" This allows the subject to report on the details.

3. Brief (i.e., one sentence) exploratory questions are asked about the relevant elements involved in the dream. Once the respondent cannot and/or does not answer one or two consecutive questions or begins to take prolonged periods of time to answer, the interviewer concludes the dream report to avoid risk of distortion, confabulation, or fantasy projection.

Each interview was taped and transcribed in order to ensure accuracy of the dream report. The transcription was examined to check for the presence of nondream material. The tape was also used to review (by an independent observer) the interaction between the researcher and respondent. The independent observer identified leading questions by the interviewer or efforts by the respondent to "please" the interviewer.

Elkan Checklist

The Elkan (1969) checklist was the instrument used for scoring the level of developmental functioning reflected in the dream content of the subjects. Elkan (1969) reported that Erikson's writings (1950, 1953, 1959, 1964) were used as the theoretical foundation upon which the checklist was formulated. According to Elkan, every description or definition of each growth crisis and its successful or unsuccessful resolution as covered by Erikson were carefully examined. One hundred sixty-eight items

were gathered, and descriptive paragraphs were written
for each of the eight growth crises; these were then trans-
ferred into questions that could be answered positively
or negatively and were used to form the checklist. Pre-
cautions were taken not to omit any of the paragraphs in
the composition of the questions. Elkan (1969) provided
her readers with the critical paragraphs, the associated
questions, and the reference from which the paragraph
was taken. The questions were then assembled in a random order.

The final compilation of questions, converted into a
checklist for the use of the judges, was used to determine
whether concerns relevant to a particular crisis were present or absent in a dream. The questions on the checklist
were deliberately designed to require a simple "Yes" or
"No" answer without allowing for any intermediate
judgments. Elkan reports that an effort was made to phrase
the questions so that the risk of interference would be
minimized.

Rating the Dream

The researcher and an independent rater scored the
dreams according to the Elkan checklist; the independent
rater was trained in the use of the checklist according to
the following format:

- The rater was informed of the study and oriented
  to the Elkan checklist by the researcher.
- The rater was given 20 identical copies of dreams
  collected by Mack (1974) in her study of emotionally disturbed and "normal" 14–15-year-olds, 10 from

each group. The rater was asked to rate them independently.

- The rater and the author then met to discuss the
  scores and compare results with Mack's ratings; the
  objective was consistency of interpretation and a
  shared basis for scoring.

Once this phase of the study was completed, the rater
was presented with an identical copy of the transactions
of the dreams collected in random order; identifying
characteristics about the dreamers were deleted. Scoring
was done independently by the raters with each of the
items on the checklist scored "Yes" or "No" in relation
to each dream. The dreams were then scored according
to the level of developmental functioning prescribed by
Elkan in her design of the checklist; the highest level of
developmental functioning rated was the level given to
that dreamer.

A second scoring system was also used in this study.
The mean score of each subject's responses was calculated. The purpose of the mean score was to examine the
results according to a scoring method that may produce
a more accurate indicator of the development functioning
of a subject's dream content. We contended that a subject's score may be inflated to indicate a higher developmental level if the highest score rated is significantly above
the majority of the subject's responses or mean score. Elkan's original scoring method was consistent with Erikson's theory of developmental growth. As a check to this
scoring system, the mean score method of rating the developmental functioning of a subject's dream content was
conducted and compared with the highest developmental
level.

Other Instruments

A measure of each subject's socio-economic status was scored by determining the education of each subject's parents. We inquired as to the highest grade or number of years of education completed by each subject's father or by the custodial parent in a single-parent family. The amount of the primary income earner's salary is also a probable indicator of a subject's socio-economic status. However, a questionnaire to parent's regarding their income was considered too intrusive for such a study and could have reduced the compliance of parents. Therefore, after consideration it was decided that such inquiries not be made.

The Amons and Amons Quick Test (1962) was used to assess the intelligence quotient of each participant. The I.Q. scores were used to determine what effect a subject's general intelligence may have had upon the results of the study. Conducting full scale I.Q. tests on each subject was considered too costly and might have reduced the compliance of parents, therapists, and subjects, particularly the emotionally disturbed group, who may have felt threatened or become defensive with any such formal and lengthy testing.

VALIDITY AND RELIABILITY

Validity and reliability concerns in dream studies have usually involved the methodological problems of dream collection and the measurement of dream content. Winget and Kramer (1979) have carefully reviewed and examined the literature on the various methods of dream collection and concluded that a number of variables account for differences in the dreams reported. They suggest that until further methodological studies of setting, method of awakening, and interpersonal situation have been conducted, it will remain difficult to compare results.

While no measurement of the reliability of recall methods as compared to laboratory awakenings for collection of dream content was found, a small pilot study (N = 30) was conducted in this study. The structured recall method for collecting dream content was employed. The results suggest a similar response consisting of important environmental stimuli, developmental tasks, and themes as reported by Foulkes (1982). Based upon this study and our experience as child psychotherapists, the structured recall method of dream content is more representative than the spontaneous recall method of dream collection. Structured recall does not constrain such research with financial, logistical, or technological realities, as is the case in a laboratory setting.

Our experience as clinical social workers specializing in the treatment of children and adolescents suggests the following: when dreams are solicited and recall is enhanced by structure, children's dream content is generally reflective of important, everyday events and memories and less indicative of bizarre or unusual events than those dreams that are spontaneously or selectively recalled. This corresponds to the findings of Foulkes (1982), who concluded that, due to the affective response of the dreamer to a frightening or bizarre dream, that type of dream is more often spontaneously recalled by the dreamer, and those dreams are disproportionate representations of all dreams experienced. The structured recall method attempts to approximate the sleep laboratory approach of recalling the dream as close to its occurrence

as possible; it provides recall of a broader, more representative array of the children's dreams.

The validity and reliability of coding systems for dream
content have been tested to a limited degree. Hall
and Van de Castle (1966) explored many of the problems
related to the reliability of dream-content measurement.
They reported that reliability is greater when the variable
to be scored is easily observable than when it is complex.
In a similar study, Winget and Kramer (1979) found that
one can expect less variance in dream study when reality-
based items, settings, or people are present in a dream
than when inferred characteristics such as anxiety or castration anxiety make their appearance. The Elkan checklist fits into the former category of content measurement
scales.

The validity of this study can be questioned by the
presence of variables other than emotional disturbance
which may affect the developmental level of the subjects.
Green (1971) reported that the cognitive development of
a particular age played an important role in the formal
structure of dreams. He added that the child with a greater
capacity for expressive ability in story-telling, imaginative
play, and daydreaming seems to have a greater capacity
for revealing dream experiences. Singer (1966) also reported that a greater expressive ability of adults in waking life is related to their descriptive ability in dream reports, despite standardized intellectual ability. Despite the
inconsistencies in the literature regarding the effect of intellectual ability upon dream reports, it appears there may
be a correlation between greater expressive ability (imaginative, story-telling, artistic ability) and an increased capacity to recall dreams and their details. Although we
found no relevant research on these observations, they

were considered important variables to take into account due to their potential to affect the results of this study.

Each subject's intellectual ability was measured by the Amons and Amons Quick Test (1962), and an estimate of his or her level of socio-economic status was determined by rating the father's highest grade completed in school. For single-parent families, the custodial parent's highest grade level completed was used. The results were calculated to determine what, if any, effect the subject's intellectual ability and the socio-economic status of his or her family may have had upon the developmental level of the dream content.

Chapter 8

Findings and Analysis

Data collected were subjected to a content analysis in relation to the two proposed hypotheses. This chapter will examine both quantitative and qualitative findings as they are sequentially presented.

HYPOTHESIS I

Quantitative Analysis

This hypothesis suggested that there were differences between the developmental level of the manifest dream content reported by adolescents with emotional disturbances and that reported by adolescents with no apparent history of emotional disturbances. Table 1 delin-

Table 1. Developmental Levels in the Dream Content of Emotionally Disturbed and "Normal" Adolescents[a]

	Developmental level								
Group	I Trust	II Autonomy	III Initiative	IV Industry	V Identity	VI Intimacy	VII Generativity	VIII Ego integration	N
E.D. adolescents			18	3	3	2	1		27
Normal adolescents			6	8	8	1	4		27
Totals			24	11	11	3	5		54

[a]The hypothesis that a difference exists in the developmental level of the dream content of emotionally disturbed and normal adolescents was statistically significant (p = .011).

Group	$\bar{X}$	SD	N
E.D. adolescents	3.70	1.17	27
Normal adolescents	4.59	1.30	27

$t(52) = 2.63$, $p = .011$

eates these results according to the rating of the developmental level of dream content of the subjects.

The results indeed confirmed that a difference existed in the developmental level reflected in the dream content of each group. The group of "normal" adolescents reported dream content indicative of developmental functioning significantly higher (or more mature) than that of the emotionally disturbed group. The dream content of 67% of the emotionally disturbed group of adolescents compared to 22% of the "normal" group was rated at Stage III (initiative) of Erikson's theory of psychosocial development, a level of development below what is theoretically expected of adolescents aged 14–16. According to Erikson (1959), adolescents aged 14–16 are expected to be functioning at a level of psychosocial development characteristic of the fifth stage: identity. Only 33% of the dream content in the emotionally disturbed group scored above Stage III of psychosocial development while 77% of the "normal" group scored above that same stage.

Eleven percent of the dream content of the emotionally disturbed group was rated at Erikson's Stage V as compared with 30% of the "normal" group of adolescents. Twenty-two percent of the emotionally disturbed group of adolescents' dream content was rated at Stage V or above, while 48% of the "normal" group was rated at Stage V or above.

Developmental scores for all subjects suggested developmental levels somewhat lower than expected for their chronological age. This may have been the result of the methodological problem of the testing instrument, which appeared to be weighted toward the lower to middle levels of development (II–IV). Elkan (1969) and Mack (1974) reported lower than expected results for all subjects tested when using the same instrument, something they believed resulted from a lower than expected socio-economic status of the subjects in their studies. The socio-economic status of subjects in this study reflected a broad representation of socio-economic levels; this should not have affected their development scores. An analysis of variance test indicated that this consideration in fact did not effect the differences between the scores of the emotionally disturbed and "normal" adolescents (P = .674). Intelligence and gender were also tested using an analysis of variance test and were not statistically significant factors affecting the results [(I.Q. = p = .172) (Gender = p = .674); see Table 2].

To examine the results in such a way that would more accurately reflect the level of developmental functioning manifest in each subject's dream content, the mean score of each subject's developmental functioning as reflected in his or her dream content was calculated. The intent of calculating the mean score for each subject was to eliminate scoring anomalies that may have occurred using Elkan's (1969) original scoring method. In Elkan's research study, each subject's dream content was scored according to the positive or affirmative responses achieved when the 144 questions comprising the checklist were applied to the transcript of a subject's dream report. Each subject's dream report was rated according to the highest level of developmental functioning scored in his or her dream report. When using Elkan's scoring procedure, a single positive score on a particular question associated with a higher developmental level would distort the subject's score if the majority of scores rated at a significantly lower developmental level. In the example given in Table 3, the individual scores of two emotionally disturbed adolescents are presented. The highest developmental level score

Table 2. *Analysis of the Effects of Gender, Socio-Economic Status, and Intelligence upon the Developmental Functioning Reflected in the Dream Content of Emotionally Disturbed and "Normal" Adolescents*

Gender

	Highest-rated level		Mean level	
	Male	Female	Male	Female
E.D. adolescents	3.75	3.71	2.74	2.49
Normal adolescents	4.78	4.50	3.24	3.10

Socio-Economic Status

	Highest-rated level					Mean level				
	S.S.	D.F.	M.S.	F	Sig. of F	S.S.	D.F.	M.S.	F	Sig. of F
S.E.S.	.53	1	.53	.31	.578	.01	1	.01	.02	.882
Groups within S.E.S.	3.61	1	3.61	2.15	.150	1.84	1	1.84	5.56	.023

F(1,47) = 2.15, p = .150   F(1,47) = 5.96, p = .023.

Intelligence

	Highest-rated level					Mean level				
	S.S.	D.F.	M.S.	F	Sig. of F	S.S.	D.F.	M.S.	F	Sig. of F
I.Q.	3.02	1	3.02	1.92	.172	1.46	1	1.46	4.93	.031
Groups within I.Q.	4.14	1	4.14	2.63	.111	1.11	1	1.11	3.75	.059

F(1.50) = 2.63, p = 1.11   F(1.50) = 3.75, p = .059

Table 3. Comparison Using Highest Developmental Score and Mean Developmental Score

| | | | | | | | VIII | | |
Subject	I Trust	II Autonomy	III Initiative	IV Industry	V Identity	VI Intimacy	VII Generativity	Ego integration	H.D.L.S.[a]	M.D.L.S.[b]
					Positive scores and corresponding developmental level					
E.D. 10	1		4	1		1			6	3.3
E.D. 17	3	4	3			1			6	2.4

[a]Highest Developmental Level Score.
[b]Mean Developmental Level Score.

and the mean developmental score for each subject are illustrated.

While most scores did not result in such dramatic differences as illustrated in Table 3, these results demonstrate the risk of inflated developmental level scores when using the checklist in the manner suggested by Elkan (1969). While the Elkan checklist is congruent with Erikson's (1959) epigenetic model, the scoring of developmental functioning by the traditional method may have distorted the rating. All of the tests on the data were calculated using both the highest developmental level and the mean developmental level for each subject. The correlation coefficient between the two scoring methods was: Pearson, $r = .66$, $p < .001$ for $N = 54$.

To calculate the mean developmental level score, a t test was used to determine if a difference in the developmental functioning manifested in the dream content of emotionally disturbed and "normal" adolescents was figured. Table 4 illustrates these results.

Data analysis using the mean developmental scores was consistent with the results using the highest developmental level scores; these verify the findings that the group without disturbances reflected a difference in the level of developmental functioning significantly higher or more mature than that of the emotionally disturbed group.

The results support the theory that there are differences in the level of developmental functioning between the "normal" and emotionally disturbed group of adolescents. The findings are consistent for either methodological approach used. These differences in the developmental level reflected in dream content clearly indicate that those adolescents with emotional disturbances will report dream content that is less mature than what would be expected. As with waking and functioning, dream con-

Table 4. Mean Scores of Developmental Levels in the Dream Content of Emotionally Disturbed and "Normal" Adolescents[a]

Group	Developmental level							$\bar{X}$	S.D.	N
	.95	2.45	3.45	4.45	5.45	6.45	7.45			
E.D. adolescents	2	18	7					2.59	0.50	27
Normal adolescents		7	17	3				3.12	0.60	27
Totals	2	25	24	3						54

[a] The hypothesis that a difference exists in the mean scores of the disturbed and "normal" adolescents was statistically significant ($p = .001$); $t(52) = 3.47$. 0–1.9, Trust; 2–2.9, Autonomy; 3–3.9, Initiative; 4–4.9, Industry; 5–5.9, Identity; 6–6.9, Intimacy; 7–8.0, Generativity/Ego Integration.

Table 5. *Lowest Rated Score of Developmental Level Reflected in the Dream Content of Emotionally Disturbed and "Normal" Adolescents*[a]

| | | | | Developmental level | | | | | | | |
Group	I Trust	II Autonomy	III Initiative	IV Industry	V Identity	VI Intimacy	VI Generativity	VIII Ego integration	$\bar{X}$	S.D.	N
E.D. adolescents	16	8	3						1.52	0.70	27
Normal adolescents	10	8	9						1.96	0.85	27
Totals	26	16	12								54

[a] $t(52) = 2.09$, $p = .041$.

tent of the emotionally disturbed group reflects developmental levels below what is chronologically expected and below that of those without emotional disturbances.

A measure of the lowest developmental level manifest in the dream content of each subject was also calculated using a *t* test to determine if there were differences between the emotionally disturbed and "normal" adolescents (see Table 5). Differences between each group were supported by that method of analysis.

This test was conducted to examine the possibility that important differences not evident in the data analysis may exist in the test results regarding the lowest level of developmental functioning scored. The results confirm and support those already achieved, that those subjects with emotional disturbances scored lower than those without such disturbances.

Hypothesis I was confirmed. Differences existed in the developmental functioning manifest in the dream content of emotionally disturbed and "normal" adolescents. Calculating the mean developmental level scores for each group and analyzing the differences between both groups not only confirmed that differences existed, but strengthened those conclusions. The results between the "normal" and emotionally disturbed groups using the mean developmental scores were higher ($p = .001$ vs. $p = .011$) than those achieved using the highest development score. The mean developmental score method also consolidated the range of scores obtained for all of the subjects and provided a more accurate reflection of a subject's developmental functioning.

Qualitative Analysis

To elaborate upon the results presented in the preceding section, a content analysis was performed.

This section will explore themes representative of each group's results. The intent of this procedure was to clarify the nature of differences found in the quantitative analysis.

The fifth stage (identity) of psychosocial development in Eriksonian theory occurs during adolescence. This stage marks the integration of identity as the individual develops personal aptitudes and experiments with various social roles. Throughout this stage, the individual is deeply concerned with the conflict between how he appears to others and how he feels about himself. It is a time when one may affiliate with a gang or clique. In the process, one may subscribe to the value system of the preferred group and have little tolerance for contradictory views or opinions, especially those of parents. Normal adolescent development is often associated with an intense need for peer supports and affiliation, from which the adolescent can begin to establish an identity separate from that of parents. Eventually, a solid sense of identity may be affirmed as integration of conflicting expectations gradually occurs. Adolescence is a prolonged stage of growth and development during which sexual identity is more firmly established, educational and vocational goals are formulated, and the sense of the individual as a separate, unique person evolves. This stage of development is generally believed to culminate with a psychological and physical separation and independence from one's parents.

The Elkan checklist (1969) included several questions pertaining to this fifth stage of development. Some selected examples included:

Question 14   Is the dreamer engaged in competitive activity with his peers in the area of occupational apprenticeships?

Question 16   Is the dreamer concerned with sta-
                   tus as reflected by dress, address, or
                   family connection?
Question 32   Is the dreamer part of a group of
                   companions in the sense of a clique
                   or gang?

These questions were oriented to issues and norms indicative of adolescent development—particularly separation
and individuation, social and vocational pursuits, and the
establishment of identity.

The dream content of many from the "normal" group
was rated at the fifth stage of development. Many subjects reported dream content consistent with Erikson's indicators. A representative dream from one subject follows:

> There was this blimp going to Ireland and I hadn't been
> on a plane like that and I was pretty scared. I felt really
> weird. I felt a really weird feeling between me and my
> mom. I just kept telling her I loved her because she knew
> the plane was going to crash. So we just kept saying . . .
> I love you, . . . I love you. . . .

Although the content of the dreams of the "normal"
group varied, the dreams were connected thematically by
an underlying concern about issues associated with expected adolescent development: identity formulation, peer
supports, and separation–individuation. The dream above
illustrated some of these themes, especially the struggle
to separate from parents. Separation is a major developmental task of adolescence, which Blos (1967) described
as the second separation–individuation stage of development. The need for this dreamer to separate was evidenced by the trip on a new type of plane never before
tried. The fear of not completing the journey was mani-

fest in the misgivings that the plane would crash and, consequently, that the dreamer would not survive the separation process. The need to remain connected to mother and the working through of that relationship were evident in the attachment between the dreamer and mother along with the adolescent's fear of separation.

Another vignette illustrated the value of peer relationships and acceptance. This was demonstrated in the following excerpt from the dream of another "normal" adolescent:

> I was supposed to go to the prom with J. and we got into a really big fight and now we are not going. We were fighting outside school in the smoking area and then came inside after the period was over. We went to our classes and then after second period I was going up the stairs and he grabbed me and said he was sorry. It was really weird because there were so many people around, like it was a big event.

The social interaction and value of sexual relationships were central in the dream of this young woman; the reaction of peers and sensitivity to social acceptance were evident. This was typical of many adolescents' primary concerns in their reported dreams.

Major developmental issues of normal adolescence revolve around boundaries, limits, and consequences of violating rules. Concern regarding social norms and the testing of these norms were illustrated by the following excerpt:

> This dream took place in Mr. B.'s [i.e., teacher's] class and I came in to his class with two beers and I asked him if I could drink them. Then Mr. J. [another teacher] comes in and Mr. B. says, "You better hide them." Mr. J. came over to me and said, "You are in a lot of trouble boy!" Then Mr. B. came over and said, "You are allowed one hour of

> drinking time per day," and I said [angrily] ". . . oh, that's
> great!"

In addition to the establishment of norms, rules, and regulations, trust issues with authority figures were themes often found in the dreams of the "normal" adolescents. These concerns were indicative of expected developmental issues and were typical of the themes in the dream content of the adolescents without disturbances.

The dream content of the emotionally disturbed group manifested themes qualitatively different from that of the group without such disturbances. The dreams of this group seldom contained developmental issues expected from "normal" adolescents. Instead, they revealed more confusing, inconsistent, and bizarre themes indicative of delayed development. The dreams of the disturbed group, as a whole, contained more chaotic and violent elements than did the dreams of the other group. Following are some examples to clarify this difference, indicative of such emotional difficulties.

An emotionally disturbed adolescent reported the following dream:

> I was on my way to school and my father was the bus
> driver: I don't know why. All of a sudden the bus just
> turned black and everything went dark. I was standing
> there for a long time, not talking or anything. After a while
> these guys came in and my father ran out and then all of
> a sudden we were back on the school bus again. When we
> got to school, we were at a pay phone trying to call the
> cops or somebody when all of a sudden the spies came in
> and pulled out a revolver and shot my father. He went
> back about 27 times.

This dream contained a number of themes typically not found in the dreams of the "normal" adolescents. The content contained more bizarre, disorganized, and aggressive qualities and was violent, hostile, and confusing, all attributes more common in the dreams of the emotionally disturbed group. The dream content of this group generally did not reveal the typical developmental issues of adolescence, corroborating the premise proposed in Hypothesis I. The violence and aggression in the dream content of the emotionally disturbed adolescents may have been indicative of the underlying conflicts related to unconscious rage and turmoil experienced by the dreamer.

Other examples typifying these primitive issues are reported below (partial reports):

> I was walking down a hallway, right? I got caught and I almost got in trouble. Then somebody saw me and they tried to put me back in my room but they couldn't. All I wanted was something to eat.

> My brother was walking alone near a graveyard. He went to an open gravestone and saw an open coffin and looked inside. He fell in and the coffin was full of nails. He tried to get out but couldn't. I tried to help but I couldn't get him out, so I ran.

> The only part I remember is that I was screaming out. I was screaming "Help! Help!" There were a whole bunch of flies all over me and I kept screaming, "Get them off, get them off!"

These dreams were typical of those reported by the emotionally disturbed group. They reflected the conflicted and tumultuous themes indicative of the developmental delays and conflicts of these subjects.

HYPOTHESIS II

Quantitative Analysis

This hypothesis predicted an association between the level of severity of emotional problems in the emotionally

Table 6. The Developmental Level Reflected in the Dream Content of Emotionally Disturbed Adolescents[a]

Level of emotional disturbance	Developmental level								
	I Trust	II Autonomy	III Initiative	IV Industry	V Identity	VI Intimacy	VIII Generativity	VIII Ego integration	N
Mild			4	1	2		1		8
Moderate			9	1		2			12
Severe			5	1	1	2		1	7
Totals			18	3	3	2		1	27

[a]Using an analysis of variance test, the hypothesis that a difference in the level of development in the dream content of three subgroups of emotionally disturbed adolescents was not statistically significant {$F(2,24) = .7606$, $p = .47831$}.

Source	S.S.	D.F.	M.S.	F	P
Group	2.12	2	1.06	.7606	.48
Within	33.50	24	1.39		
Total		26			

Table 7. Highest Rated Level of Development for the
Emotionally Disturbed Adolescents

Level of emotional disturbance	Mean score	SD	N
I. Severe	3.43	.78	7
II. Moderate	3.58	1.16	12
III. Mild	4.12	1.45	8

disturbed group and the developmental functioning re-flected in dream content.

The subjects were placed into three categories of emotional disturbance: severe, moderate, and mild. (See Appendix D for a complete description of the symptoms associated with each category.)

Table 6 presents the ratings of the level of developmental functioning reflected in the dream content of the three categories of emotionally disturbed adolescents. Results attained using the highest level of developmental functioning method for scoring did not show a statistically significant difference among the three groups of emotionally disturbed adolescents.

The results did, however, reveal that the majority (66%) of emotionally disturbed subjects' dream content was rated at a level reflective of Erikson's third stage of developmental functioning (initiative), a stage much lower than would normally be expected for adolescents 14–16 years of age. Of those emotionally disturbed adolescents whose dream content was reflective of developmental functioning above the third stage of development, 78% were mildly or moderately disturbed. This suggested that a trend did exist in the data indicating that clinical differences exist between the three groups of emotionally disturbed adolescents. Although the hypothesis that a dif-

ference would be found in the level of developmental
functioning reflected in the dream content of the three
subgroups of emotionally disturbed adolescents was not
statistically supported, an important relationship was found
between the level of diagnosed emotional disturbance and
the developmental level reflected in dream content as
proposed. The small sample size and statistics used in
this study reduced the power of the statistics and increased the risk of rejecting a true hypothesis. The risk of
a type II error in rejecting the hypothesis (that significant
differences existed in the dream content between the various levels of diagnosed emotionally disturbed adolescents) was a possibility. Increasing the sample size in future studies of this type is suggested. Cowger (1984) writes
that the distinction between the theoretical significance as
compared to the statistical significance in evaluating research should not be overlooked, and careful qualitative
analysis of the data and its clinical relevance should be
conducted.

When the mean score for each of the three subgroups
of emotionally disturbed adolescents was calculated, the
level of developmental functioning reflected in dream
content decreased as the severity of emotional problems
intensified. The results indicated that the more disturbed
or severe the level of emotional problems, the more delayed or immature the developmental level reflected in
the dream content. Table 8 presents these findings. Those
subjects with emotional disturbances categorized as severe were rated lowest in the developmental level reflected in dream content. The data suggested that a relationship consistent with Hypothesis II existed between the
developmental level in dream content and emotional disturbance. The moderately disturbed adolescents scored the

Table 8. Mean Scores Rated for Levels of Development for the Emotionally Disturbed Group

Level of emotional disturbance	Mean score	SD	N
I. Severe	2.38	.60	7
II. Moderate	2.59	.39	12
III. Mild	2.78	.57	8

next highest level of developmental functioning in dream content and the mildly disturbed group rated even higher. As predicted, the normal group of adolescents were ranked at the highest level of developmental functioning in dream content among the subgroups.

The mean score of developmental functioning reflected in dream content of disturbed adolescents also was calculated. A statistically significant difference in their scores was not found. A relationship was found, however, between the level of emotional disturbance and the mean developmental score reflected in dream content. These results are presented in Table 9.

The results of the mean scores of developmental functioning did not reveal a significant difference between the three groups of emotionally disturbed adolescents. Despite the lack of statistical significance, the results indicate that important clinical differences existed which suggested a relationship between the level of emotional disturbance and the mean developmental score reflected in the dream content.

The lowest mean developmental scores for any of the emotionally disturbed subjects were for those in the severely disturbed category. Two (or 29%) of the severely disturbed group had mean developmental scores be-

Table 9. The Mean Scores of Developmental Levels Reflected in the Dream Content of Three Categories of Emotionally Disturbed Adolescents[a]

Level of emotional disturbance	Developmental level							
	0.1–0.9 Trust	1–1.9 Autonomy	2–2.9 Initiative	3–3.9 Industry	4–4.9 Identity	5–5.9 Intimacy	6–6.9 Generativity	7–7.9 Ego integration	N
Mild			6	2					8
Moderate			9	3					12
Severe		2	3	2					7
Totals		2	18	7					27

[a]When using the mean level score of each subject, the results are not statistically significant: {$F_{(2,24)}$ = 1.1143, p = .34551}.

Source	S.S.	D.F.	M.S.	F	P
Group	.56	2	.28	1.1143	.3445
Within	6.09	24	.25		
Total		26			

tween 1.0 and 1.9 on the Erikson scale, while none of the moderately or mildly disturbed group had developmental scores less than 2.0.

The mean scores for each of the three subgroups of emotionally disturbed adolescents were calculated with results supporting the findings that there were important trends in the developmental level reflected in the dream content of emotionally disturbed adolescents. The mean scores for all of the subjects with severe emotional disturbances were lower than the mean scores for the other two groups; the moderately disturbed adolescents reflected dream content scores higher than the severely disturbed group, but lower than the mildly disturbed group. These trends lent clinical support to the second hypothesis proposed in this study: that the more severely disturbed the emotional problems—indicative of psychologically delayed developmental functioning—the more delayed or immature the developmental functioning reflected in dream content.

Intelligence, socio-economic status, and gender were not statistically significant factors effecting the results. That the differences in dream content were the result of various levels of intelligence among the subjects, or that economic or class differences produced distinctions, or that males and females reported differences in dream content were unfounded. None of these factors had any significant influence upon the results. Differences in the developmental level of the dream content were the result of the presence or absence of emotional disturbances.

Qualitative Analysis

Content analysis showed that developmental functioning reflected in the dream content of severely emotionally disturbed adolescents was more delayed or immature than that of the moderate or mildly disturbed subgroup. This finding was consistent with the developmental-psychology theory that diagnosed that emotional disturbances reflect developmental delays and that symptoms are manifestations of those delays. The results of this study supported the notion that dream content was reflective of developmental differences existing between emotionally disturbed and "normal" adolescents (i.e., the less mature the intrapsychic development, the less mature the level of developmental functioning reflected in dream content).

Other thematic differences in the data indicated that those adolescents with more severe emotional difficulties reported dream content with more primitive, disturbed, and violently aggressive qualities than those with less severe disturbances. Those adolescents with mild emotional disturbances reported dream content more closely resembling that of normal adolescents. The dream content of the mildly disturbed adolescents contained more themes of peer relationships, social interaction, and separation–individuation than those of the severely disturbed group.

Table 10 is a list of primitive developmental themes reported in the data; the number of emotionally disturbed subjects reporting incidents of bizarre content and/ or excessive hostility is also reported. Forty-three percent of the severely disturbed and 58% of the moderately disturbed adolescents reported dream content reflective of primary elements and themes. While the percentage of primitive themes was greater for the moderately disturbed group than for the severely disturbed group, this was most likely a reflection of the variability and fluidity found in the subjects' symptoms. Combining the severely

Table 10. *Primitive Developmental Themes*[a]

Level of emotional disturbance	Number of adolescents reporting bizarre content and hostility			
	Y	N	N	%
Severe	3	4	7	43
Moderate	7	5	12	58
Mild	1	7	8	12
Normal	3	24	27	11

[a]Presence of excessive violence, bizarre content, and extreme hostility in the manifest dream content of the emotionally disturbed adolescents.

and moderately disturbed subgroups resulted in 53% reporting primitive developmental themes as compared with the 12% for the mildly disturbed; this supported the view that differences existed in the quality of dream content reported for those with different degrees of emotional disturbance.

Table 11 (mature developmental themes) examines the presence of positive peer and social interaction, characteristics more indicative of expected adolescent development; the number and percentages of emotionally disturbed adolescents reporting those themes in their dream

Table 11. *Mature Developmental Themes*[a]

Level of emotional disturbance	Number of adolescents reporting incidents of positive peer and social interaction			
	Y	N	N	%
Severe	1	6	7	14
Moderate	4	8	12	33
Mild	4	4	8	50
Normal	13	16	27	48

[a]Presence of positive peer and social interaction in the manifest dream content of the emotionally disturbed adolescents.

content are reported. The results show a clear progression in the frequency of more mature, age appropriate developmental themes as the level of emotional disturbance becomes less severe. These results supported the notion that those with less severe emotional disturbances reported more mature dream content, resembling that expected for "normal" adolescents. Only 14% of the severely disturbed adolescents reported dream content with incidents of positive peer and social interaction as compared with 50% of the mildly disturbed adolescents.

Examination of the dreams reported by adolescents with different levels of emotional disturbance provided examples of the divergent themes in dream content reported. For example:

> There was this fight between me and a friend. I remember really distinctly that a kid hit me and I fell down four flights of stairs. It was like floating and I zoomed right up to him and started beating him. Then he stabbed me and I'd get right back up, you know, and I'd stab him; you know, it was like a never-ending battle.

This adolescent was placed in a residential program for boys with emotional disturbances and was reported to have disorganized thoughts and vivid fantasies, was physically aggressive to others, and had an extremely low-level of self-esteem. His dream content revealed primitive themes with references to violence and aggression, repetition, continuation of a difficult struggle, and defense of body. These issues were consistent with Erikson's earliest stages of developmental functioning (Elkan, 1969).

The primitive quality of dreams in the emotionally disturbed group was evident in the following dream:

> I was walking in a dark forest and got lost. I was looking around, you know, to see if anybody would find me. So I just kept on walking and walking and walking, then I came to see the Red Forest . . . and I'm standing there and I

hear a voice and it said, "You're in the Red Forest." I looked around and couldn't see anybody. I was so scared I started running and running and then I fell and twisted my ankle. I fell asleep and when I woke up the next morning, a unicorn was standing next to me with a nice long white mane. It said, "Get on." I got on top of it and we started riding and all of a sudden we came to this big cliff and I said "Stop!" and it wouldn't stop and I said, "My God, we're going to fall!" The next thing I know, wings come out and we start to fly! We keep on flying around and around. Then they told me I had to leave and I said, "I ain't leaving you." Then I said, "Why don't I just stay with you?" It said, "You can't," and I said, "Yes, I can, you watch." I stayed for a while and we became good friends and it showed me rainbows and its world . . . then, all of these little white unicorns came around and I said, "I want to stay here. Don't make me go back," He said, "No, you have to go back," and I said, "I don't want to!" After that they said, "Okay, you can stay," and then I woke up.

In reality, this adolescent suffered from symptoms of rage, self-destructive behavior, occasional disorganized thought, splitting of the object world, and multiple substance abuse: symptoms indicative of a borderline personality disorder. While gentle and benign in theme, the dream contained issues of isolation, dependence on others, holding onto or controlling others to attain one's needs without reciprocity, which, developmentally, are all characteristic of severe difficulties in attachment or preseparation from parents and typical of immature disturbances. This subject, whose symptoms were indicative of a severe emotional disturbance, reported dream content with developmentally primitive and immature themes.

SUMMARY

These findings supported a number of conclusions regarding the dream content of adolescents. The first hy-

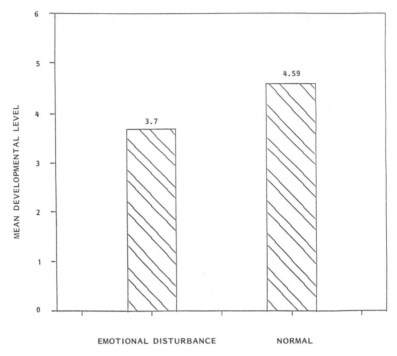

Figure 1. The mean developmental level rated in dream content by the normal and emotionally disturbed groups using the highest developmental level rating scale methods.

pothesis tested confirmed the findings of earlier studies that developmental differences existed in the dream content of "normal" and emotionally disturbed adolescents. Qualitative analysis showed that adolescents with emotional disturbances reported dreams with primitive qualities: more bizarre, aggressive, and hostile themes. Those adolescents without emotional disturbances reported dreams with more mature qualities, displaying themes typical of normal adolescent development: positive social and peer interaction, separation–individuation tasks, and vocational or educational concerns.

The mean developmental scores of each subject were calculated in order to reduce inflated developmental scores and to provide a more accurate measure of developmental functioning reflected in the dream content. The mean scoring method strengthened (.001) the results produced in testing Hypothesis I using the highest developmental level scoring method (.11).

Hypothesis II—that an association existed between the level of severity of emotional disturbances and the developmental functioning reflected in the dream content—was

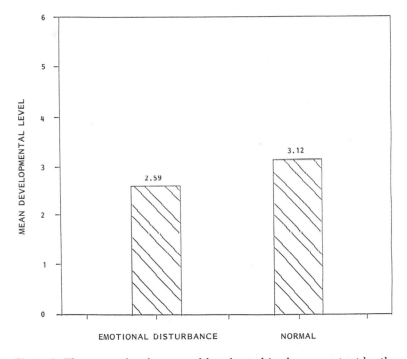

Figure 2. The mean developmental level rated in dream content by the normal and emotionally disturbed groups using the mean developmental rating scale method.

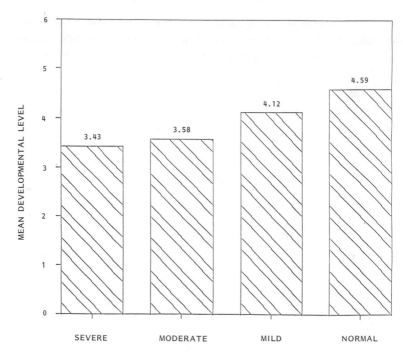

Figure 3. The mean developmental level rated in dream content by the three subgroups of emotionally disturbed adolescents using the highest developmental rating scale method.

not supported. Although neither the original scoring method (highest developmental level) for the Elkan checklist nor the mean developmental level scoring method provided statistically significant results, the latter more closely approached a level of significance (p = .34) than did the highest developmental level method (p = .76).

Qualitative analysis revealed significant themes that clinically supported the hypothesis:

- A relationship among the three subgroups of emotionally disturbed adolescents was found, indicating that the level of developmental functioning reflected in dream content decreased as the severity of emotional problems intensified.
- The mean score of developmental functioning in dream content for each subgroup of emotional disturbance decreased from mild–moderate to severe. These results were consistent for both the highest

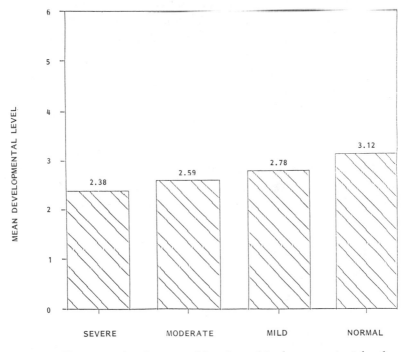

Figure 4. The mean developmental level rated in dream content for the three subgroups of emotionally disturbed adolescents using the mean developmental rating scale method.

developmental level and mean developmental level
methods of scoring.

- Adolescents with more severe emotional disturbances reported a greater amount of bizarre content and excessive hostility than those with mild
  emotional disturbances.
- Adolescents with mild emotional disturbances reported a greater number of positive peer and social
  interactions than those with severe emotional disturbances, characteristics associated with normal
  adolescent development.
- Thematically, adolescents with more severe emotional disturbances reported more primitive, disturbed, or bizarre dreams than those with mild
  emotional disturbances.
- Limitations of the study include the small sample
  size, methodological problems with the scoring instrument, and difficulty in operationalizing and en-
  suring normalcy.

A summary of the results of the test of the first and
second hypothesis are graphically displayed in Figures 1,
2, 3, and 4, using both the highest developmental score
and the mean developmental score methods of measurement.

Part IV

Theoretical Implications and Practice Techniques

Chapter 9

Contributions to Dream-Content Theory

The relevancy of the following criteria and their implications for clinicians, researchers, and educators will be explored and elaborated upon in this chapter:

- First, the findings of our study contribute vital data to the research on dream content and its meaning. The study reinforces the use of developmental theory as a means by which to understand dream content and the ego-adaptive aspects of human behavior.
- Second, the results indicate that dream content is a useful therapeutic focus for clinicians. The results offer empirical data which utilize dream content to help understand the important thoughts and issues

of the adolescent as well as help to learn more about the emotional conflicts they may exhibit.

- Third, this study suggests important issues related to clinical education: the role of dream content analysis and research in clinical practice, and the role of the therapist as a researcher and contributor to practice theory and techniques.

DIFFERENCES IN THE DREAM CONTENT OF EMOTIONALLY DISTURBED ADOLESCENTS

These criteria indicate that this study was the first to advance the research of Elkan (1969) and Mack (1974) in establishing a developmental continuum for the dream content of children and adolescents. The data identify a difference between the developmental functioning reflected in the dreams of emotionally disturbed children and that reflected in the dreams of those without emotional disturbances. The work of the authors noted above and of the other significant contributors to the study of dream content has established a new perspective from which to view dream content and expand its practical and clinical uses. The longitudinal studies of dream content and the association between dream content and normal developmental functioning have moved dream-content analysis away from a highly speculative, interpretive psychoanalytical perspective. This theoretical shift utilizes the knowledge gained from recent advances to incorporate the physiological aspects of cognitive functioning and memory-processing into understanding dream content. These changes have added a new dimension to the understanding of dreams. By incorporating the longitudinal studies of broad samples of children's dreams—not just those selectively remembered or collected from samples of children's psychotherapy—the knowledge of children's dreams has expanded considerably.

These trends have produced a new school of thought that conceptualizes children's dream content not as undisguised wish fulfillment, but as the ego's attempt to integrate events and memories of everyday life. The tasks involved include the developmental issues the child is attempting to process (Ablon & Mack, 1980; Foulkes, 1982). Elkan (1969) first established a developmental scale, based on Eriksonian theory, for rating the dream content of children and adolescents, and hypothesized that developmental functioning was reflected in dream content. Mack (1974) first applied these results to test the differences between the dream content of emotionally disturbed children and adolescents and the dream content of those without emotional disturbances. Her results indicated that differences between the two groups of adolescents existed.

The first hypothesis in our study is the only known effort to re-examine the research conducted by Mack (1974). Methodological changes in the collection and the rating of the dream-content reports were incorporated to improve the reliability and validity of Mack's (1974) study, providing a more precise assessment of developmental functioning as reflected in the dream content of the subjects.

THE ASSOCIATION BETWEEN DEVELOPMENTAL FUNCTION AND DREAM CONTENT

The theoretical basis for the second hypothesis of this study builds upon the research of Elkan (1969), Mack (1974), and Foulkes (1982). They concluded that dream content was reflective of developmental functioning, and hypothesized not only that emotionally disturbed adolescents reflect delayed developmental functioning in their dream content but that the level of delay was associated with the severity of their emotional disturbance. The hypothesis suggested that those from the emotionally disturbed group, with symptoms indicative of early developmental delays and conflicts, would report dream content reflective of early developmental functioning. Those with emotional disturbances whose symptoms and associated diagnosis reflect more mature developmental functioning would report dream content reflective of more mature or higher developmental functioning.

The trends established in the findings suggested that differences existed in developmental functioning in the dream content of emotionally disturbed adolescents with various levels of emotional disturbances. Those with the most severe emotional disturbances reported dream content of the lowest level of developmental functioning. Emotionally disturbed adolescents with mild emotional disturbances reported dream content reflective of developmental functioning higher than those with severe or moderate disturbances and closest to that of normal adolescents. The qualitative analysis supported the trends that those with severe emotional disturbances reported dream content with the most primitive or bizarre themes, while those with mild disturbances reported more mature dreams that reflected developmental functioning closer to what would be expected of normal adolescents.

There may have been important factors contributing to the lack of statistical significance in the results of Hypothesis II. In view of the nature of this type of research, it is important to evaluate such contributing factors and their effect on the study. Methodological problems encountered in the research may have influenced the results, the most important of which included the Elkan checklist (1969), the instrument used for measuring developmental functioning reflected in dream content.

The checklist, comprehensive in its attention to the Eriksonian theory of psychosocial development, was, nevertheless, not without its limitations. One area of concern was related to the questions themselves. Elkan (1969) paid a great deal of attention to developing questions that would capture the critical elements of Erikson's psychosocial stages of development. In addressing that issue, the author failed to be specific enough in her use or interpretation. For example, question 120 ("Does the dreamer believe that he can depend on others to provide what he needs?") caused confusion in the minds of the independent raters as to its meaning. An uncertainty developed as to whether or not this question was inquiring about the dreamer's positive dependency on others to provide what he or she needed or if the question was addressing the dreamer's ability to trust others in a mature interpersonal manner. Because the developmental level associated with each of these two interpretations of the same question is discrepant, it can affect the score a subject receives. By including more specific instructions regarding the scoring of certain questions that seem to imply the presence of a characteristic or trait, the methodology could be improved. Similar problems were found in question 43 ("Does the dreamer feel comfortable with his own body?") and question 48 ("Does the dreamer need to be needed? Is he pleased to be needed?"). Both of these questions required that the raters not score them affirmatively unless the observation was consciously addressed or otherwise indicated by the dreamer. Thus, an implication of a characteristic or trait in the dream report alone was not sufficient to score an affirmative response.

Finally, other methodological changes also may improve the reliability of the instrument. Requiring its use over a period of time with a number of dreams per subject is a possibility. Collecting many dreams from subjects over an extended period of time may provide a more comprehensive view of developmental functioning. This method, rather than the single dream method, would allow an examiner to more fully and, perhaps, consistently assess a subject's level of developmental functioning. The benefits of an extended period of data collection of dream content would assist in comprehending aberrant scores achieved by a subject in a single dream. This would be particularly useful in understanding developmental regression in dream content. By learning what environmental situations or stressors result in changes in the developmental functioning of a subject's dream content, one may learn more about the individual's reaction to conflicts and the regression he or she is likely to experience. Conversely, changes in dream content indicating developmental progression may provide some insight into the events or circumstances in a subject's life that promote adaptation and growth.

THE USE OF CLINICAL PRACTICE AS THE LABORATORY SETTING

This study demonstrated that the clinical practice setting was a viable alternative to the laboratory as a site for conducting research of this type.

Clinical practice affords security, comfort, and trust as a result of the therapeutic relationship formed between clinician and patient. Such rapport is not cultivated in the technical laboratory setting. This therapeutic relationship is particularly important in reporting dream content of an unusual, conflicted, or sensitive nature. Clinical practice settings—rather than the impersonal laboratory setting in which dream content is reported to a technician—offer the advantages of an interpersonal relationship between therapist and client that may provide for disclosure of more disturbed, conflicted dreams. The clinically based therapeutic relationship also provides the added advantage that the dreamer, with the assistance of the therapist, can begin to associate to the dream. This remains the most important mode of interpreting dream content. This process enhances the therapeutic relationship as both client and therapist together engage in understanding the meaning of the dream.

The study of dream content has moved from theoretical origins based upon case studies to the laboratory and now back to the clinical setting where research findings can be applied. This study integrated an accepted clinical theory (developmental theory) with the study of dream content. By accomplishing these tasks, the data and their usefulness become more available to clinicians.

REVIEW AND SUGGESTIONS FOR FURTHER STUDY

These findings support the view of dream content as an adaptive process that emphasizes the problem-solving, mastering characteristics of the dreaming ego. Emerging theory in the field of dream research parallels that already established in the larger sphere of psychotherapeutic literature regarding the emphasis upon ego psychology rather than instinctual psychology of the unconscious. Theoretical emphasis on the adaptive, problem-solving aspects of dream content has slowly developed within the past 15 to 20 years and has been evident in the literature and research regarding children's dream content throughout the past 10 years.

The influence of developmental ego psychology and child-development theory within the past 30 years has resulted in an emphasis on adaptation and the sequential progression of developmental tasks and processes. The results have stimulated the conceptualization of children's dream content as reflective of important memories and coping mechanisms and as indicative of developmental tasks and the functioning of the dreamer.[1]

By eliciting the dream reports of child and adolescent clients and viewing them from a developmental perspective, the clinician may become more attuned to their level of developmental functioning. These data are valuable resources for assessing the level of developmental functioning and identifying the relevant issues or conflicts that may be contributing to emotional problems. In ongoing therapy, the therapist may monitor a client's level of developmental functioning by exploring dream content. The clinician may evaluate the intensity of developmental conflicts, assess the effectiveness of therapy in resolving those difficulties, and learn about the client's developmental progress throughout treatment.

Given the changes in cognitive functioning and abstract thinking, adolescents usually find dreaming and dream content an interesting and unusual means of communicating. The majority of the "normal" and emotionally disturbed adolescents in this study found dreams exciting and of great interest. Dreams offer a unique mixture of egocentric thoughts, memories, and associations, yet there is a defensive quality as well; a form of displacement seems to occur, making dreams less threatening to

[1]See Chapter 5 for further details.

talk about. Because dreams maintain a distant, external quality as something that "happens to us," or is "coming from outside" our consciousness, they may be easier to discuss with a clinician than conscious thought. Dreams can be particularly valuable in the assessment or treatment of an anxious or resistant adolescent who may have difficulty discussing issues that are conflictual. Some adolescents, reluctant to acknowledge difficulties with unresolved developmental conflicts, may find their dreams intriguing and discuss them in treatment.

By establishing that a difference in developmental functioning exists in the dream content of emotionally disturbed adolescents, the clinician has available another method for assessing the developmental functioning of a client. The analysis of a dream report no longer need be limited to psychoanalytical interpretations based on wish fulfillment or repressed drives, but can be used clinically to understand the developmental issues or tasks confronting the adolescent. Dream recall and its use in psychotherapy also enable the therapist and client to establish a dialogue that enhances therapeutic communication. Previous research (Ablon & Mack, 1980; Green, 1971) reported that enhanced ego-functioning was achieved through dream recall. Through the process of dream recall and the associations to dreams in psychotherapy, the client gains the experience and benefit of exploring important thoughts, wishes, and memories. Because dreams have a fascinating appeal, particularly to the adolescent who may be developing a cognitive capacity for abstract thinking, the interest in associating to dream recall may be a valuable resource to help the client engage in the therapeutic process.

Dreaming helps to process important memories, wishes, and thoughts about people and events. Adolescents' dreams incorporate these issues in a way that reflects their level of developmental functioning. In this way, dreaming tends to enable the adolescents to integrate the circumstances and events of their lives in a developmentally coherent manner, a process similar to ego-functioning in wakefulness. Dream recall and the associations to the dream enable adolescents to use their ego-functioning to understand the meaning of the dream, its relevance to issues of concern to them, and their thoughts and feelings about those issues. Dreaming is an adaptive process incorporating those thoughts and issues: "thinking" during sleep. The use of dream content can be utilized effectively in diagnostic and continuing psychotherapy to reveal more about the client, his or her level of developmental functioning, and the ongoing process of therapeutic change.

Other populations need to be studied in order to expand knowledge about developmental functioning in dream content. No studies have been conducted, with adults, that utilize developmental functioning as a model for understanding dreams. Developmental functioning reflected in the dream content of latency-aged children has been conducted by Elkan (1969) and Foulkes (1982). Although Mack's (1974) findings were inconclusive, she suggested that dream content of emotionally disturbed latency-aged children was different from that of "normal" children of the same age. Methodological difficulties were believed to be contributing factors in producing Mack's (1974) inconclusive results. The cognitive and verbal skills of preschool or early-aged children make them a less likely population in which the functioning of dream content can be firmly established. More can be gained, however, by studies of the developmental functioning reflected in the dream content of latency-aged children and adults, as well as that of adolescents. The study of the dream content of various ethnic groups and social classes can also provide valuable information about the differences in psychosocial processes and developmental tasks related to these factors.

A survey of clinicians focusing on their knowledge of research and use of dream content in clinical practice would be another suggestion for further study. Dream content is still largely associated with the psychoanalytical perspective, emphasizing instinctual drives and repression, which hypothesizes dream content as unconscious wish fulfillment. This framework regards the latent content of the dream as an indicator of unconscious thoughts and relies upon symbolic interpretation as a means to understanding the dream. As a result, dreams have been rendered theoretically important, but functionally impractical or "off-limits" to many clinicians. While dreams are listened to and perhaps explored, they may be used infrequently in clinical practice, except in psychoanalysis or psychoanalytical psychotherapy. Without an awareness of the more recent advances in and approaches to understanding dream content as an indicator of developmental functioning, a valuable therapeutic technique as a means to understand the client may be lost.

Chapter 10

Clinical Applications and Techniques for Use in Practice

ENHANCING DREAM RECALL

The use and application of dream content in clinical practice with children and adolescents are unclear and ambiguous to most therapists. Although no empirical data exist to verify the assertion, the extent to which dream content is used in treatment is largely dependent upon the background, experience, and comfort of the clinician. The interest and fascination of the child or adolescent in dreaming are important considerations and likely contributors to his or her ability. The mention of a dream by a client provides the therapist with a heightened sense of interest and anticipation. Expectations of hidden traumas, conflicts, or neurosis as revealed in dreams await the therapist, along with an uncertainty regarding the meaning of dream content or its use in practice. It is as if many therapists are aware or assume the importance of dreams reported in treatment, yet are unaware of how to facilitate their use and application in practice. Many therapists still assume that psychoanalytical training in dream symbolism is required in order to apply dream content to clinical practice. This chapter will discuss the application of dreams in clinical practice with children and adolescents.

One of the first considerations is the collection and use of dream content in clinical practice. Because of the previously noted difficulty in remembering dreams, efforts must be made to improve dream recall and incorporate the procedure in the usual clinical practice techniques. Children who find dreams interesting and like to remember or discuss them spontaneously will most likely reveal a greater ability to recall their dreams. If children are creative or expressive artistically, verbally, or emotionally, they will most likely also remember more dreams—and in greater detail. Children and adults can be taught to enhance their own dream-recall ability. When encouraged to think about and remember their dreams, children display an increased ability to do so. When a trusted, caring adult is attentive and interested in a child's dreams, the child's own interest is enhanced and his or her recall ability improves over time. The child tends to remember more of his or her dreams, often with increased clarity and detail. Since memory capacity is diminished during sleep and dreaming, the stimulation, interest, and practice of reporting dreams early the next morning or day will improve the dreamer's ability to recall the content and detail of dreams.

In psychotherapy, where an effective relationship between client and therapist is absolutely essential and considered by many to be the single most important curative factor, dream recall can be encouraged and effectively facilitated. Since dreams represent our "thinking at night" and reflect important memories, events, developmental tasks, and wishes, they provide an excellent vehicle for discussion and expression in treatment. An effective rapport between client and therapist can be developed or enhanced with the discussion between the therapist and client of the latter's dream content.

Therapists do not require the psychoanalytical training in dream symbolism or the experience and training in psychoanalysis to use dream content in clinical practice. Awareness by the therapist of dream content as an indicator of developmental functioning, ego-functioning, important events, and memories, and the interest in utilizing dreams in clinical practice are essential for effective use in psychotherapy. The clinician and his or her client must engage in the interest and discussion of dream content in order to promote its effective use in treatment.

Younger children (ages 5–6 to approximately 11–12) are frequently referred to treatment for behavioral difficulties at home and/or school, poor academic performance, and occasionally for more internalized disturbances such as depression, anxiety, or phobic symptoms. The therapeutic process is often confusing and unclear to the child. A variety of effective modalities and techniques exists in the diagnosis and treatment of young children with similar complaints or disorders. This author usually relies on an initial session or two with parents alone to acquire the necessary background data: family, developmental, social, academic, and medical history, and other important information related to the child, family, and the problem. The child is then seen alone for up to, but usually not exceeding, five visits. This provides an initial assessment of the child's functioning, the underlying dy-

namic formulation associated with the problems, as well
as much information as possible related to the child's ego
strengths and psychological developmental functioning.
It is during the first session with the child that the process of treatment is explained and reviewed. An introduction to the therapist and a discussion of the reason
(symptoms and concerns of parent or reporting agent) for
the referral as well as of the nature and purpose of working together are conducted at this time. This information
is often reviewed throughout the course of the assessment and occasionally throughout the entire treatment
process. A variety of variables influences this process of
course, such as the chronological and developmental age
of the child, intellectual capacity, the defenses employed
by the child, transference reactions, the nature of the
problem, and the course of treatment. It is during this
initial assessment that the process of treatment is discussed and reviewed with the child. Issues related to
confidentiality, and the behaviors, moods, and feelings
associated with the problems that affect or confront the
child and his/her family are discussed at this time. This
culminates with a treatment plan discussed and reviewed
with parents and the child. Clarification of this process
leads to the cooperation and engagement of the child in
the treatment process—a critical and essential component
of treatment.

   It is during the initial assessment phase that the clinician attempts to understand the child and the nature of
the conflicts that affect him, while simultaneously attempting to engage the child to participate in the treatment alliance. At this time, the process of treatment is
explained to the child: how child and clinician will talk
and play to better understand the child's feelings and
moods. This child is told that sometimes children feel the

way he or she does (e.g., "sad," "mad," "angry," "scared") because of feelings and it is explained that they will work together to better understand, cope with, or change those feelings, moods, and/or behaviors. Discussion is held at this time regarding the estimated duration of treatment, the frequency and length of sessions, as well as confidentiality, protocol (if any) of treatments, and other related items or issues. Play activities with younger children are reviewed as well as any "ground rules" regarding what is or is not acceptable behavior or activity for the session (i.e., leaving the office during a session; use or misuse of the therapist's personal items; hurting people or self).

Play, games, drawings, and story-telling and their use in treatment are discussed as are dreams. Dreaming, when explained to the children, is referred to as our "thinking during sleep." Children are asked if they ever dream and if they ever can remember any of their dreams. If they can or are eager to recall a dream, the clinician is encouraged to listen attentively and react appropriately as he or she would with any verbalization, fantasy wish, memory, or play theme that a child at this age may have. Clearly the content, both manifest and latent, is important and may serve as a crucial indicator of the child's central conflicts or transference reaction to the therapist. The dream as reported at that time may serve as a defensive quality and be seen in a global or projective way as a reaction to treatment. A differentiation is noted at this time between manifest and latent content of dreams, a distinction detailed in previous chapters. For practical use, the detail, events, and developments of the dream as remembered are considered the manifest content. It is the manifest content of the dream that is seen as reflective of developmental functioning and conflicts as well as an indicator of important memories, events, and wishes. The latent content represents the child's own understanding, meaning, or associations he or she ascribes to the dream, as well as that which remains unconscious or is not remembered. Seldom does a child, particularly a younger child or one new to the therapeutic process, make associations to the meanings of dreams. Yet if a child can verbalize as to what he or she feels a dream may mean, an important therapeutic insight may be achieved.

SCHOOL-AGED CHILDREN

The initial discussion regarding dreams and dream content, however, is usually intended to familiarize the child with the process and role of dreams rather than to elicit any significant dream recall. More often than not, young children respond with a shrug of the shoulders or no awareness or recall of dreams when initially asked about dreams. It is at this time that the clinician can effectively introduce and promote interest in dreams and dream recall. A brief discussion of dreams as a normal part of sleep usually begins the procedure. Many younger children (5–7 years) often tend to exhibit some reluctance in acknowledging or recognizing dreams as distinct entities, probably due to the cognitive difficulty in clearly distinguishing dreams from the fantasy, play, or projection that occurs at this age. The clinician can help the early latency child become familiar with the nature and process of dreaming by briefly reviewing that dreams occur at night to everyone. It is helpful to the child to hear that it is usually difficult to remember dreams very well the next morning and that dreams sometimes are "strange, funny, and weird and don't make any sense. Sometimes things happen in dreams that could never really happen when we are awake and sometimes they are scary, too." It is helpful for the young child to know that dreams are at times characterized by "frightening monsters, strange creatures, big animals, or even mean people who chase us or are after us." These explanations help to reduce the fear and guilt the child may experience in dream recall and to lower the inhibitions that "they are the only one who has such scary dreams." Such feelings usually produce some guilt or anxiety in the child that he or she somehow is responsible for or associated with the quality of the dream experience. This discussion and review helps to reduce any fears that the bad or scary dream is the result of some misbehavior or is punishment for certain actions, deeds, or thoughts.

The notion that dreams are a useful part of the therapeutic process is introduced to the child during this beginning phase of treatment. As the assessment or diagnostic formulation is occurring and the child is introduced to therapy as a process that uses thoughts, feelings, and play to "help understand problems and worries in order to make them better, dreams are included as important components of this process, representative of our thoughts, feelings, and wishes at night." The interest, concern, and ability to understand the child and his or her problems or worries and help make them better are the foundation of the therapeutic alliance between child and clinician regardless of the modality or orientation employed. The introduction and use of dream content in the therapeutic process should occur at this time, with the therapist's interest in all of the child's thoughts and feelings, whether they occur at day or night. The child should perceive the therapist as interested and wanting to know about any thoughts or feelings that may be frightening, a source of anxiety or guilt, or otherwise a concern for the child. Any communication or discussion (waking thoughts, fantasy, projection or dream content) regarding issues, thoughts, or feelings of the child help to establish a therapeutic alliance.

Dream content is of added importance because of its use as an indicator of developmental functioning and conflict. The manifest content of the dream as a reflection of the developmental functioning/conflicts of the child is a valuable diagnostic and treatment technique for the therapist to employ. Much like behaviors, symptoms, interpersonal relations, and intrapsychic functioning, dream content can be used as an important indicator of the developmental level and conflicts of a child. In addition, important memories, events, or behaviors are also reflected in the child's manifest dream content and can likewise be useful to the therapist in learning about what is important to the child and occupying his or her thoughts and attention.

The latent content of the dreamer is of more interpretive or associative value in treatment. Therapeutically, dreams are most useful if the dreamer can associate to "what the dream may mean" to him or her. This reflective property promotes self-disclosure as well as self-awareness and insight regarding those issues confronting the dreamer. Most children, however, are unable to process and associate to dreams in this fashion. This process is more likely to benefit the therapist working with adult or verbal and insightful adolescents. Occasionally, however, an insightful and unusually mature and verbal latency-aged child may be able to make some useful associations to the meaning of a dream and its relevance to him or her. In such cases, the clinician must consider that the child may be using intellectualized defenses in responding to such questions with such insight.

Following the early introduction regarding dreams and their use and place in "our work together" (e.g., therapy), the child is told in whatever manner or terms most applicable and comprehensible that the therapist is interested in his or her dreams. The therapist informs the child that he or she would like to learn more about the child's dreams, that dreams can be useful in helping to understand the child's problems or worries, and that they can be used to help make these problems better.

A reminder or brief explanation about how dreams are easily forgotten is very useful to solicit the child's motivation and compliance with the method for collecting dream material. The child is asked to place a pen or pencil and some paper next to the bed at night. As soon as the child awakens he or she is asked to write and/or draw anything remembered about the dreams of that night. The child is instructed to keep each dream separate and write (or draw) as much detail and information about each dream as can be remembered. Once again, reminders regarding the difficulty remembering dreams and the possibility that the child may not be able to remember any dreams are helpful in easing any anxiety or guilt the child may tend to experience with an assigned task. Young children, as well as adolescents at times, are told they can make up a dream to report if they wish. This allows the child who cannot remember a dream to comply with a request and participate in the process without fabricating. The "made-up" dream provides the therapist with important projection, fantasy, or wish material.

If the child is comfortable with the request, he is asked to bring in his dreams to the sessions. Not all children are comfortable, compliant, or organized enough to do so. While all children can be asked and assisted to use their dreams in treatment, not all will or can. Parents can be of assistance in gently reminding the child to put paper and pencil next to the bed at night, but caution must be taken. Not only can the process be contaminated, but an added stress or burden can be placed upon the child by the parent who overly or rigidly demands the child comply with the doctor's or therapist's request. The clinician must carefully assess parents' ability to effectively assist or remind the young child about the procedure. Any concern that parental involvement in dream-recall procedures may produce conflict or tension should be recognized, and the parents should not be involved in the process. If doubt persists regarding parents' ability to refrain from the process, then the likely effect upon the child and the procedure should be examined in order to determine whether the procedure should be avoided or not. In either case, an important family or parent–child interaction is evident, which can be of considerable diagnostic or treatment implication. The standard therapeutic principle of "above all, do no harm" remains most useful and is certainly applicable in dream content. If the therapist has any concern that even this simple procedure may cause difficulties related to compliance or parental relationships, it should be avoided.

Children are asked to bring their dreams with them to their sessions. At times, a designated notebook or drawing pad is a helpful motivator for children to keep their dream material. The notebook also serves as an incentive and enhances the "special" qualities or properties of the dream collection. The timing of requests or inquiries regarding dream content needs to remain flexible. The therapist's style and manner, along with the child's own ease, interest, and motivation in reporting dreams, must be taken into account. Dream reports are best integrated into the customary flow of therapy. Often, sessions with children begin with a discussion of news or information concerning important events that have occurred since the previous treatment session. Dream reports can be elicited at this time. Questions such as "Have you had any dreams you remember since our last visit?" or "Can you tell me about any dreams you wrote down since our last session?" are direct and clear to the child. The therapist responds to an affirmative reply with interest and a request to hear the dream or dreams of the child. Similar to the structured recall approach noted in previous chapters, the therapist can assist recall by asking a question or two concerning the details of the dream. The following example will help demonstrate the process:

> A seven-year-old boy was in treatment due to indications he had not resolved his feelings concerning the accidental death of his older brother. His brother, who was seven at the time of his death, was hit by an automobile while playing outside his home with his younger brother (the client), who was five at that time. The boy was asked if he remembered any of his dreams since our last visit. He shook his head affirmatively and reported the following: ". . . I was in a big dark forest and saw something which looked like a bear with a human face. I just stared at it and every time it moved, giant scorpions came out of its face." Pause followed by a question from the therapist: "Was anybody else there with you?" "No, I was there by myself. I was in the woods behind my house near the tree–fort." Therapist: "What tree–fort?" "The tree–fort behind my house that me and my mother and some friends built." Therapist: "Do you remember anything else about that dream?" "No." After a

> brief pause the boy was asked by the therapist: "What
> do you think about that dream?" The boy said noth-
> ing and shook his head indicating he didn't know.
> He was then asked "What do you think it [dream]
> may mean?" He replied after a brief moment: "Scary."

Indeed, the dream was scary to him, and he could draw no associations or meaning from the dream content to his own life. The meaning of the latent content can possibly relate to the frightening and dangerous quality of the area near his home. This young boy has reason to perceive his home as a potentially dangerous place. While he appears to be doing well and has few symptoms or manifestations of unresolved grief, guilt, or other distress, he verbalizes very little and is somewhat closed emotionally at home and in treatment. (This dream was reported during his third session.) Associations regarding the identity of a bear-like creature with a human face, which he did not recognize, and the scorpions coming out of its face lead to speculation concerning his deceased brother. The fort near which this event occurred remains an uncertain source of security, which may be precisely what this young boy experiences. The appearance of the frightening and threatening creature may be related to the guilt he may also be experiencing.

Primarily because of the age of this child and his lack of introspective thought, latent content must be inferred from dream material by the therapist. This is often the case with such young children. The manifest content of the dream, however, can be of important value as well. In his dream, this young boy is frightened by an unknown creature in the woods near his home. Frightening figures, monsters, or creatures are often experienced in play, fantasy, or dreams by early latency-aged children between the ages of 5–7. The dream occurs near his home and in the absence of others. He neither avoids the creature nor defeats it in any way, but rather is subject to its terror as he observes it. Developmentally, the dream indicates some minor psychological delay of the dreamer. The content of this dream may typically be expected from a child within the 5–6 year level of development. Using the Elkan checklist (1969) as an indicator of developmental functioning, this dream is reflective of developmental functioning characteristic of Erikson's third developmental stage: initiative versus guilt.

In addition to its developmental value, the dream helps facilitate communication between the boy and the therapist. Although the client is rather closed to his emotions and without much affect, the exchange and dialogue between him and the therapist regarding such content and the attempt to understand its meaning are valuable facilitators of therapeutic communication. The child and therapist together can explore the occurrence of frightening and scary thoughts (e.g., dreams) and try to understand their meaning and importance. In this way, the frightening thoughts, feelings, and experiences of the child are safely discussed in a therapeutic process, leading toward further exploration, discussion, and understanding. Dreams serve functions similar to play or fantasy for the young child. The manifest content can often be utilized in a projected or displaced fashion to understand the reactions, emotions, or motivations of the child as well as his or her developmental functioning. This provides the therapist with a greater understanding of the child and can lead to further insight and awareness of issues or conflicts affecting the child directly.

Another latency-aged (eight-year-old) girl was seen for approximately 10 sessions for issues related to her biological parents' divorce and her adjustment to her mother's remarriage. This girl was experiencing an adjustment disorder related to her changing role and status within her custodial (mother's) family. Her mother had recently given birth to her second child within two years from her present marriage with the client's stepfather. The child was clearly feeling displaced and alienated from her mother, with whom she had been extremely close and mutually dependent, especially during her mother's unhappy marriage and subsequent separation and divorce. She no longer felt important to her mother, now preoccupied with a new husband and two infants.

During approximately her third or fourth session, she reported the following dream:

> A little duck lived by himself in a small house below the ground. The duck was sad because he was having a very bad day. He spilled his drink because the glass was so full. Then the ice cream fell off his ice cream cone and later when he was eating all the picks [i.e., tines] fell out of his fork.

This dream was marked by obvious symbolism and reference to her own self-image. Like the duck in her dream, this young girl was feeling sad about her perceived lack of status and place within her family. She, too, felt as if everything she did went wrong. Unlike many young children at this age, she was able to report to her therapist that she "felt like the duck sometimes." She then proceeded to verbalize her sad feelings because of the time and care provided to her two younger siblings. In addition, with some minor assistance, she was able to examine her symptomatic behavior at home and school in relation to these feelings. Her unusual ability to articulate her feelings so clearly enabled rapid success in family treatment sessions to occur; the problems decreased, and her treatment was successfully terminated.

ADOLESCENTS

As with many therapeutic and nontherapeutic issues alike, adolescents present unique characteristic qualities and dilemmas. Two fundamental principles concerning treatment of adolescents consistently emerge in the literature as well as in practical application and clinical experience. The first essential component regarding effective treatment of adolescents concerns the knowledge of the dynamic process of adolescent growth and development (Blos, 1962, 1970; Farnsworth, 1966; Group for the Advancement of Psychology, 1968; Offel, 1969, 1975; Piaget, 1959, 1962). The developmental changes and normative crisis accompanying adolescence involve physical changes, the onset of sexual development and activity, separation and individuation from parents, and the establishment of autonomous social, vocational, cognitive, and emotional functioning. These varied and dynamic developmental processes are critical in order to understand adolescents and young adults. Recognition of the unique technical aspects of psychotherapy with adolescents is the other essential property in effective treatment with this age group. Psychotherapy with adolescent clients requires that the adolescent client be successfully engaged in the therapeutic process. The quality of the relationship between client and therapist is paramount in this process (Josselyn, 1971; Masterson, 1967, 1972; Meeks, 1971). In order to maintain the relationship, the therapist must be adaptive and responsive to the particular needs of the adolescent client. The setting of the treatment and approach used by the therapist must at times be flexible enough to be conducive to the adolescent, thus fostering and promoting trust in the relationship. While true for all clients, adolescents in particular require trust and security in the therapist and the therapeutic relationship.

Dream content can be an effective and useful method to engage adolescents in the therapeutic process while providing insight into their developmental functioning. Often adolescents who may be reluctant or difficult to engage in treatment find dreams fascinating to think and talk about. Finding themselves in a period of cognitive development during which the advent of abstract thinking occurs, adolescents frequently engage in thought, debate, and arguments concerning concepts and moral dilemmas previously never considered. Dreaming is a phenomenon not well understood and marked at times by unusual and bizarre events and occurrences. Dreams often appeal to adolescents because of their unusual characteristics. Our research with normal and emotionally disturbed adolescents frequently has demonstrated their acute interest and fascination with dreams and with the meaning of dream content. Many adolescents are interested in the properties and meaning of dreams, often with a desire to know if dreams are predictive of future events, contain hidden properties or messages, or are indicative of certain characteristics of the dreamer.

Because of this interest in dreams, many adolescents can be easily engaged in remembering their dreams and participating in the structured dream-recall exercises. They find dream content a useful means for projecting unacceptable thoughts and impulses. The events, developments, and emotions contained in their dreams are easier for adolescents to relate to and speculate upon than their own thoughts and feelings. Much like play, fantasy, or other projective techniques in treatment, speculating upon and relating to dream content is easier and less threatening to the adolescent than self-disclosure and introspection. Because dreaming and dreams are not easily understood, often unusual or illogical, and hard to integrate, they are safer to speculate about and explore. They can also serve as a source of displaced affect and emotion for the adolescent dreamer, which he or she can more easily relate to in treatment. Adolescents often will find it easier to share their feelings and thoughts concerning the events or characters in their dreams than the reality of waking life. This is often true even if they are the central character in their dream. It is easier for the dreamer to maintain a distance or sense of independence from dream content because there remains a feeling that the dream is "happening" to the dreamer, that he or she is not responsible for the content; this makes it easier to associate to and speculate upon than real events occurring during waking hours.

Adolescents often find the process of relating to dream content interesting and challenging, while not threatened by its implications to their own thoughts and feelings. Such dialogue allows the adolescent and therapist to mutually explore the events and experiences within the dream, as well as the feelings of the dreamer, in a nonthreatening fashion. Doing so enables the client and therapist to learn about the adolescent's feelings and reactions to certain events or people occurring in his or her dream; it also assists in determining the adolescent's developmental conflicts and level of functioning. This therapeutic dialogue can be expanded to include the adolescent's own thoughts and views (e.g., associations) regarding the dream, which can be used to help the dreamer understand those critical events or conflicts he or she faces in waking life.

The underlying latent content and any associations the adolescent can make to that dream material can be successfully employed in treatment with adolescents. However, because the majority of adolescents are developmentally, socially, or psychologically not as prepared or likely to use psychotherapy in an uncovering fashion, such benefits and use are not as likely to occur. This, of course, is dependent upon the particular client involved; those adolescents who are prepared for and engaged in insight-oriented or uncovering types of psychotherapy can be encouraged to use dream content in this fashion. More likely, however, is the use of the manifest content of the dream as a means to learning about what events, people, or developmental issues are important to the adolescent. The discussion and understanding of the people, events, and issues that appear in dreams can be used by the therapist and adolescent as a framework for establishing a therapeutic relationship and a treatment alliance.

One adolescent female who was seen in individual outpatient therapy and family therapy for a combination of hystrionic and depressive symptoms reported the following dream:

> I was walking, and I don't know where I was going but I was walking, and then I was in this room. And I was watching something up on a wall, then people started coming into the room where I was and then we started to talk. Can't remember what we were talking about but I think it was something about, bragging about what we can all do and would like. All these people could do something really good or really bad. This one guy, I think it was an old guy, an old guy that was a man, huge, dark hair—that's all I remember, he walked over to this girl. She was really skinny, light brown hair, and then he slammed her against this table, round table. Then after that she just went "ugh" and then she jumped right back up again. Then I was reading something in some weird language. It didn't make any sense, but I could pick up the words but I didn't know what they were saying.

This sixteen-year-old was the product of a highly dysfunctional family and had a number of social difficulties with her peer group, despite being a good student academically. Her behavior was seen as disruptive and attention seeking at home and school, and she alienated many of those around her. She felt unaccepted at home and school because of her behavior and her excessive weight. She and her mother were constantly arguing and rejecting one another.

The dream she reported in approximately her 10th session is characterized by developmental issues related to competence and achievement. The attempt to prove herself is evident by the bragging in which the people in the dream engage and the acquisition of skills not fully integrated or understood by the dreamer. The violence inflicted by an unknown male upon a "skinny" girl likewise is related directly to this obese adolescent's concern regarding her size and associated fear of rejection.

A mean level rating of this dream according to the Elkan checklist (1969) placed this adolescent at Erikson's third stage of psychosocial development—initiative versus guilt—two stages below the stage that would normally be expected of an adolescent: identity versus repudiation. The manifest content of this dream was an avenue the adolescent could use to explore her feelings regarding her size and the rejection she experienced at school and from her mother.

CONTRAINDICATIONS AND OTHER CLINICAL USES

Experience suggests that there are few clinical circumstances or situations with children or adolescents in which the exploration and use of dream content is not advised. There appears to be no reference in the litera-

ture indicating any psychic danger or risk involved in using dream content in clinical practice with such clients.
Certainly our own experience in the use of dream content
for both data collection and clinical practice reveals no
evidence of emotional conflict, regression, or distress for
any children or adolescents.

Of particular concern in our research for such contraindications where those severely emotionally disturbed adolescents who were in psychiatric inpatient settings and carried psychotic, severe affective, or personality
disordered diagnosis. Concerns regarding the fear of regressive reaction or a psychotic episode for such clients
were warranted: recalling and verbalizing a free associative process such as dreaming may not produce the structured recall process of remembering dreams; reporting
dreams may actually result in regressive behavior or disorganized thought process. Follow-up contact with clinicians or staff of all of the emotionally disturbed adolescents in the study revealed not one reported account of
any disturbance or conflict attributed to the dream-recall
activity for any subject.

Our clinical experience also confirms that dream recall does not promote or produce any intrapsychic disturbance or conflict. However, much like other uncovering
or introspective techniques not indicated for clients with
a fragile ego or otherwise easily prone to highly disorganized or chaotic thought processes or behavior, structured dream recall in treatment may not be indicated. The
process of recalling and reporting a dream—that may
contain emotionally charged, unusual, or bizarre content
and is reflective of primitive developmental functioning—
for those children with severe emotional disturbances must
be carefully evaluated. Because so few younger children
present with highly disorganized thinking and with the

use of psychotropic medication to aid in the management of the symptoms associated with severe disturbances, many clinicians treating children are unlikely to encounter such clients, particularly on an outpatient basis. Careful assessment of the potential clinical risks and benefits associated with dream recall must be undertaken prior to use with any emotionally volatile client. If a child or adolescent is experiencing difficulty controlling his or her emotions or is troubled by distressing or delusional thought processes affecting his or her ability to function, structured dream-recall techniques are not advised. The risk that recalling and reporting dream content may exacerbate the already severely impaired thought processes of such a child exceeds any likely benefits. Any therapeutic technique that may threaten the psychic structure of a client or otherwise promote disorganized thought should be avoided. Those children and adolescents with severe emotional disturbances who are experiencing stress or difficulty in their thought processes are not likely to benefit from structured dream-recall techniques at that time.

The use of dream content with severely disturbed children and adolescents can still be of significant therapeutic value in treatment with such clients, however. If children with severe emotional problems are engaged in a therapeutic program and treatment effectively modifying thinking disturbances and assisting in emotional health, dream content can be a helpful adjunct in treatment. Dream content can be successfully utilized in treatment of even a severely disturbed child if the necessary structure and supports are available. It can assist the therapist in learning about the reality-based issues concerning the child or adolescent, as well as the level of developmental functioning of even those severely emotionally disturbed. The use and discussion of dream content can also be used to facilitate effective therapeutic communication between the severely disturbed child and the therapist if employed in this fashion.

Therapists treating children and adolescents with less severe emotional disturbances need to be aware of the potential to use dream-content discussions to avoid or deny other conflicts. Although intellectualization as a defense is more likely with adults than children, those children wanting to avoid conflicts in this manner may use dream content to do so. Because of the quality and content of dreams, they can provide a wealth of material which a client prone to such defensive techniques can use in treatment to avoid or distract himself from the issues troubling him most. There also may exist a tendency among therapists who are most interested in dream content to unintentionally aid in such avoidance or resistance by inadvertently collaborating with the client's defenses. Therapists must constantly process for themselves the course and results of treatment and the methods utilized.

It is encouraging to see the recent discussion of varied uses and applications of dream content in clinical practice. Discussions of dream content as a method of access to the pattern of early mother–child relationships and as a means to promote self-discovery now can be found in recent literature (Beck, 1977; Edward 1987; Lucente, 1987). The implication of such discussion suggests that dream content can be effectively utilized in a variety of clinical applications Such discussion and debate must continue to expand the use of dream content in clinical practice.

Much more work remains to be done in understanding dreams and the process of sleep and dreaming. An integration of physiological, cognitive, and psychological knowledge and skills must continue in order to maximize our understanding of dreams and their meaning. No longer are the data of dream content in clinical practice constrained by those few dreams spontaneously recalled and reported by clients in treatment or exclusively limited to psychoanalytical interpretation and use. A much broader empirical base now exists, which has greatly influenced our understanding of what children dream about. This has provided insight into the dreams of children and adolescents with emotional disturbances and how they differ from those without such disturbances. Those differences can now be understood within a developmental context and effectively utilized in diagnosis and treatment.

Dream content analysis is one of the many techniques that help establish therapeutic communication between client and therapist. Dreams provide a wealth of useful material about the issues, feelings, and memories most important to the child.

The chapters that follow will provide some useful examples of dream content and its uses, and suggestions to help parents understand their children's dreams.

Part V

Normal and Emotionally Disturbed Children's Dream Content

Chapter 11

The Latency-Aged Child

Below are some examples of the dreams of latency-aged children, ages 6–8, with no known history or indication of emotional disturbances. These dreams depict the usual and customary events of these children's lives and are characteristic of the dream content of this age group.

The dream of a 6-year-old boy:

> I was playing in my yard with a friend. We were playing in a fort and fighting like Indians.

One 6-year-old girl reported the following dream:

> [I had a dream] that we were going to Disneyland. Mommy, Daddy, and my sister got on the plane and landed in Disneyland. We went on all the rides and had a lot of fun.

Another 6-year-old recounted the following dream:

> I was sitting in my kitchen and all of sudden everybody
> came in with a big cake and sang "Happy Birthday." We
> had lots of cake and ice cream and I didn't even know it
> was my birthday.

Occasionally, young children will report dreams of unusual, strange, or bizarre events. These dreams are also quite common, particularly for younger children. Dreams of this type are consistent with this age group's use of fantasy and projective play, and often symbolically represent the child's developmental tasks of coping with an expanding social world and of focusing on learning and achievement.

An 8-year-old boy's dream:

> There was a monster with big, huge horns on its head
> chasing me down the road. It was ugly and mean but I
> ran into my house and I was safe.

A 7-year-old reported this dream:

> I had a dream that I won a trophy that day for BMX rac-
> ing. I was so happy and everybody thought I did great.
> While we were all asleep, a robber came in the house and
> stole my trophy, which was on the table next to my bed.
> When I woke up it was gone. I was sad.

The following dreams were reported by latency-aged children in treatment. Following the dream report, a brief description of the child and of the meaning of dream is given.

An 8-year-old girl who was being seen because of excessive fears and anxiety recounted the following two dreams:

> I dreamt there was an earthquake. Everything in the house
> fell and I didn't know what happened.

> I was putting away my pillow and suddenly I am being

> lifted up and I don't know how. I yell for Mom who didn't
> hear me, then I just woke up.

This young girl was experiencing anxieties because of her fear of losing her mother. The family had recently experienced significant losses through the death of a grandparent and a close friend. Although no symptomatology to warrant a diagnosis of separation–anxiety was evident, this 8-year-old nevertheless feared the loss of her mother. She was able to express her concern only through displaced fears and anxieties at home, news accounts, or other symbolically associated sources.

The exchange, discussion, and explanation of the fears she experienced in her dream enabled the therapist to diagnose her problems and developmental conflicts more precisely. This helped her to trust the therapist and disclose her worries and fears in a safe, supportive environment. Together they were able to extrapolate from her dream content her associations to her mother and effectively reduce her anxieties.

A 7-year-old boy was being seen in treatment in order to help him cope with his feelings and behavior regarding his foster placement, precipitated by the chronic neglect and abandonment by his mother. He reported the following dream:

> I was in the woods at night and being chased by twenty
> monsters. They were running after me and I was all alone.
> They didn't catch me because I ran in the house and they
> tackled my mother. I took a knife and cut their heads off.

This boy's dream reflects many of the fears and anxieties often associated developmentally with younger children, approximately 5 years of age. The dream also characterizes his anger and rage at his mother, as well as the guilt he may experience because of his feelings toward her. His dream was diagnostically useful to his therapist and was one of the few avenues available in treatment to assist him in processing his feelings regarding his mother.

Chapter 12

Dreams of Adolescents

A 13-year-old adolescent who loved baseball and played regularly reported the following dream:

> I had a dream that they moved Fenway Park next to my house. I was the only one allowed to go in and play any time I wanted. It was awesome.

A 16-year-old adolescent girl recounted this dream she had recently:

> My ex-boyfriend picked me up. He came over my house and we got in his car and were just sitting there because I left my makeup in the house and I didn't have any on. I told him I wasn't going anywhere until I got it and he wouldn't let me out of the car. We were just sitting there in my driveway and I kept saying "I need my makeup" and he said "you don't need it that bad."

A 16-year-old boy described a dream he had recently:

> I was at a place that I had applied [for a job] which was a
> restaurant. For some reason, I was lined up with other
> people and they were telling me I didn't fill out my appli-
> cation right. It wasn't complete. They kept telling me I
> wasn't going to get the job.

One 17-year-old boy reported the following dream:

> I was with H., S., K., and T. We were in class together
> and somebody yelled "Hey there is weed [marijuana] in
> the front row." So we went down and had some, then K.
> started yelling at us to get out of the room, so we did.
> Next thing I remember is walking around the neighbor-
> hood smoking [it].

These dreams represent those reported by adolescents without emotional disturbances. They reflect a sampling of the social and developmental issues affecting adolescents. Beginning with the youngest of these teenagers,
the 13-year-old boy's dream depicts his most important
interest and passion at this time in his life, baseball. He
maintains the wish and desire to play major league baseball which, regardless of his ability, is indicative of a developmental level consistent with his relative immaturity
when compared to the older adolescents. The dream content of the 16–17-year-olds accurately reflects the variety
of developmental issues occurring at that stage of life. Social and peer influences, sexual interests, vocational and
educational pursuits, and evolving moral development and
experimentation are among the issues confronting older
adolescents.

In comparison, the dreams that follow are reported
by adolescents with emotional disturbances who were in
active treatment at the time the dreams were reported.

One 16-year-old adolescent with a serious emotional

illness requiring psychiatric hospitalization described the following dream:

> The President was coming to my house. When he walked into my room I had a bucket of gas and some matches. When he walked in the room, I set the room on fire and gas spilled on him and he blew up.

A 14-year-old adolescent girl, who was in an inpatient psychiatric hospital and categorized by her therapist as having a moderately severe emotional disturbance, narrated the following dream:

> I was driving on a truck with my boyfriend. We were going down this long, thin, dirt road. On one side was a big cliff and stuff. We were driving around and this great big truck is heading right toward us and it's about to hit us and I wake up. Then I'm back asleep and dream it all over again.

Another 14-year-old psychiatric inpatient who was characterized as experiencing a moderately severe emotional disturbance reported the following dream:

> Well it was weird 'cause I didn't really understand it. I kept like, you know, I was just like wow, is this weird. I was like going from place to place, I don't know how I was getting there or what I was doing. I was like, first I was at the retreat, then I'd be home or supposedly home, and then I'd be at my grandparents' trailer or something. Then I'd be here again, and all these different people. It was really weird how I was getting from place to place and everything.

This adolescent's dream was rated as developmentally immature: Stage II of Erikson's psychosocial development, autonomy versus shame and doubt. The alienation, lack of security, and confusion concerning his location appear to reflect his insecurity and lack of attachment with others. The difference in this dream from those previously reported by the adolescents without emotional disturbance confirms the varied levels of development.

Within the emotionally disturbed group, a clear distinction is seen between the dream content of those with severe emotional disturbances and those with minor difficulties. Those differences support the theoretical position and the results of our study. That position asserts that, as with developmental theory, a continuum exists in the dream content of those whose functioning and symptoms reflect delayed emotional growth and maturity. The examples that follow are two dream reports from adolescents who were in outpatient treatment for what were catagorized as mild emotional problems.

The first dream is that reported by a 14-year-old in treatment for adjustment and behavioral difficulties:

> I think it was two nights ago that D. said that I couldn't smoke any more. And I guess it was so much that I dreamed about, I had a dream that I was smoking a cigarette and D. said "Hey" and I said "What" and he said "Put that cigarette out and you're grounded for a week." And I got mad and I had an attitude. I just, I woke up that's what I remember.

Another dream reported by a 16-year-old girl:

> I'm in a red jeep and driving forward. All of a sudden the jeep starts going backwards. I had no control over it. It was speeding by itself. I remember stepping out of the jeep and I didn't even get hurt. When I got out it was so strange, as if I was floating. I stood on the ground and saw my mother beside me, looking straight ahead. When I turned to look at her I got a little closer and found that the jeep had hit a brick wall and was smashed up into nothing. If I didn't get out in time I may have been killed.

These two dreams are more similiar in theme and developmental content to those of adolescents without

emotional disturbances than to those with severe disturbances. Theoretically, this is what would be expected from
adolescents whose developmental functioning is mildly
delayed or disturbed, as compared to those whose symptoms and diagnosis are indicative of significant developmental delay.

Chapter 13

Dreams of Children with Specific Problems

SEXUALLY ABUSED CHILDREN

The following dream was reported by a 17-year-old:

> I was in this white room with nothing in it. You know sort of blank and empty and nobody and nothing in it, it was totally empty except for these white walls. I was dreaming that he was coming after me and I just couldn't get away. [I] kept getting away and getting away, trying to keep myself from him. I remember waking up with all sorts of scratches on my face where I kept clawing myself, trying to make myself ugly so he wouldn't touch me.

A 16-year-old boy who had been sexually abused at least twice in his life described the following dream:

> I had a dream I was with my friend and we spent the day together. He came over my place and we played some

games and did some things together and went out to the
lake. We had a good time and came back to my house, ate
supper and he spent the night. He was up in my room
and we exposed ourselves to each other as well as fondled
each other. Then he and I were sort of making out on the
bed and then I woke up.

Each of these dreams reveals themes and concerns of
those who have been sexually abused. The first dream,
that of an adolescent who had been sexually abused by
her father as a child, revealed the bleak emptiness and
isolation she experienced as well as the attempt to deny
her sexuality to the abuser. Her issues are ones frequently shared by many abuse victims.

The adolescent male who was abused years ago by a
much older adolescent reveals the questioning of his own
sexuality in his dream. While sexual identity is an important issue for many adolescents to question, this boy's
experiences and victimization have contributed to his uncertainty. His dream content provided an opportunity to
discuss sexual identity issues confronting him in a displaced and safe fashion. It was easier to talk about the
dream and his associations prior to discussing his own
experiences and feelings.

The following dreams were reported by a 4-year-old
boy who had been sexually abused by his adolescent
brother:

I had a dream that I was in the middle of the water all
alone, drowning. I was calling and yelling for help but
nobody heard me. Then I woke up.

I was with my Mom in a big shopping center and we got
lost from each other. I couldn't find her. There was too
many people. Then I started to cry and get real scared.

These dreams were reported within one week of the disclosure of the second incident of abuse by his brother

within an eight-month period. The dreams reflect the regressive developmental fears of danger and abandonment often experienced by children who have been sexually abused. The trauma of the repetitive abuse this boy suffered is also evident in the similar themes of both dreams, in which he is exposed and subject to danger without parental protection.

MEDICALLY ILL CHILDREN

Frank told me about a dream where he was out playing in his backyard. All of a sudden a giant chicken came out of the woods behind his house and towards him. The chicken chased him and with its large beak was about to bite him on the arm, when all of a sudden his father came out of the house and shot the huge chicken dead. The doctors told him he would be okay and that his father should bring him back if this happens again.

Frank's dream indicates that he is coping very well with any fears and feelings of guilt that may be associated with his illness. In his dream, he is saved by doctors and is predicting his likely need to continue treatment: in the dream the doctors say that if this were to happen again, all he would need do is have his father bring him back and the doctors would make him better once again. Here Frank seems to be anticipating just such a necessity and reassuring himself that no harm will come to him. His dreams are helping him to learn to cope with the stress brought on by his illness as well as helping him to learn to deal with his worries beforehand, reassuring himself that he will be all right. In addition, we see how Frank is also using his father to assure his safety. In fact, this boy's dream allows him to derive the benefit of the added security of his father's protection. The dream also suggests that if for some reason his father were actually unable to be the direct source of comfort or protection as he was in the dream, the boy has the capacity and willingness to use others to help him adapt to and cope with his fears. A 19-year-old young man who a few years prior suffered a serious head trauma resulting in numerous physical complications (most of which he has recovered from) and some residual emotional, behavioral, and personality difficulties reported the following dream:

> I dreamt I was in this idealistic, spectacular, and beautiful house and everything was just right. I heard some noises and it occurred to me that somebody else was there with me. I wasn't scared by the noises and kept on living there and enjoying myself.

The dream reflects this adolescent's continuing concern with understanding and coping with the effects of his head trauma. The "idealistic, spectacular, and beautiful place" in his dream represents his association to his life prior to his head injury. The "noises" that he could neither identify nor understand are representative of the cognitive and emotional confusion he experiences from his head injury—perhaps analogous to "noises in his head." The dreamer's association to the dream was that he "isn't frightened of those things he cannot understand." While the dream's content accurately reflects the issues surrounding his functioning, the dreamer utilizes denial of the central conflicts confronting him. Developmentally the dream also reflects the primitive and delayed stages of isolation, fear, and understanding at which the client is functioning.

CHILDREN OF DIVORCE

Children cope with divorce according to a variety of factors. Critical among them are the support systems in place, parents' attitude and ability to relate to one another, gender differences, and stage of development at the time of separation and divorce. Dream content of children who are attempting to cope with or adjust to parental divorce will often reflect some of the developmental insecurities associated with their age. One 7-year-old boy whose parents had recently divorced reported the following dream, which describes his concerns with remarkably clear symbolism:

> I dreamt that Daddy surprised us and was over our house at Christmas. We opened gifts together and had lots of fun. Then all of a sudden he put us in the car and we left. I don't know where we were going but we were mad because all of our gifts were at Mom's house. We were crying.

This dream is indicative of the conflict and turmoil experienced by a young school-aged child whose parents have recently divorced. The wish for parental unification as well as the anger, frustration, uncertainty, and confusion about the events or circumstances confronting him are quite evident.

A 10-year-old girl whose parents were divorced and who was living with her father, stepmother, and three younger siblings from her father's remarriage reported the following dream:

> There was a little puppy who had a family that loved him very much. But the family had three kittens who didn't like the puppy. They were mean to him and hurt his feelings so he ran away. He was sad but was happy again when his family found him and brought him home.

This dream reflects the displacement this young girl felt as the only child from a previous marriage. The manifest content reveals her fear of rejection by her parents and isolation from her younger siblings, often seen in blended families. The dream helped her integrate her parent's love for her and begin to consciously identify and address her worry and fears.

Part VI

Helping Parents Understand Their Children's Dreams

Parents are often very interested in and concerned about their children's dreams. While they are usually unsure as to what the dreams mean, many often seek to know as much as they can and to do what they can to help, particularly if their child has experienced a nightmare or suffers from frequent disturbing dreams. This final section is intended as a guide for parents who are involved in treatment with their child or are otherwise interested or curious about children's dream processes.

This information can serve as a useful tool for the therapist in a number of ways. Parents who know about dreaming and dream content can help facilitate dream recall with their child. Because of the need to employ the structured dream-recall techniques at home, parents can be very helpful in supporting and assisting these efforts.

Perhaps more importantly, learning more about the development issues children confront throughout childhood and adolescence can provide parents with an increased awareness of and sensitivity to these critical issues in their child's life. Knowing more can better prepare adults for the complex and challenging task of parenthood. Discussion of dreams and the feelings they bring also can promote communication between parent and child about these important issues. Children will experience their parents as interested, caring, and concerned about what they think. Parent and child alike can benefit from the exchange of thoughts, feelings, and ideas.

Below is an outline of the topics covered in Chapters 14 to 18.

Chapter 14   Introduction for Parents

Chapter 15   What Are Dreams?
                Learning about Sleep
                Dreaming
                When do Dreams Begin?
                Distinguishing Dreams from
                    Fantasy and Daydreams

Chapter 16   What Do Dreams Mean?
                What Children's Dreams Mean
                Developmental Issues
                Different Dreams at Different Ages

Chapter 17   What about Nightmares?
                What Do Nightmares Mean?
                Why Do Children Have
                    Nightmares?
                Night Terrors

Chapter 18   Techniques for Parents
                     Techniques to Improve Dream
                         Recall
                     Communicating about Dreams

Chapter 14

Introduction for Parents

A 6-year-old girl reported a dream in which she was running through the woods by herself when all of a sudden she ran into a big tree. She hit the tree so hard an apple fell down. The apple started speaking Spanish to her and began running around and around the tree. She felt happy and began to sing and dance with the apple.

A 14-year-old adolescent told of a dream he had in which he was standing in his high school gym all dressed up in a tuxedo. He was standing next to a door like a guard. Suddenly through the wall crashed a big, clear balloon with a beautiful woman inside whom he did not recognize.

He started chasing the huge balloon across the gym, outdoors, and across the parking lot of his

school. The balloon drifted upward and met a U.F.O.
that swallowed the balloon and quickly disappeared
from sight.

These are but two examples of the wonderful world of
children's dreams. From the beginning of time, dreams
have been a source of interest and fascination and continue to be so today. Dreams are often unusual, sometimes frightening, and always interesting. This is particularly true when it comes to understanding the dreams
of children.

Children's dreams are full of wonderful images of
singing apples, dancing houses, and friendly unicorns who
carry children on their backs through billowy clouds and
across rainbows. This enchanted dream world, however,
also contains a darker side as well. Strange ferocious
beasts, killer sharks, and unusual happenings are also part
of every child's dream world.

What do these dreams mean, and does the presence
of frightening events or figures indicate that a child is
experiencing a problem? What about the disturbing reoc-
curring dream? Should parents be worried, and what can
they do to help? The answers to such questions can be
found in the children's dreams themselves. While children may not be able to describe verbally the important
events and developments in their lives or the meaning of
these events, their play and dreams often reflect what the
child is unable to say with words.

With parenthood necessarily comes the nighttime activities of raising children: nightly feedings and diaper
changes, sitting up with a sick child, and answering the
cries for mommy and daddy by a child jolted awake by a
terrifying dream. The impact of such a dream can be as
disquieting for the parents as for the child. Concerned

parents interested in what their child dreamt about listen attentively as the child describes his or her traumatic experience, and attempt to comfort the child. Parents, however, often are uncertain and sometimes anxious about their child's dreams. They fear that dreams of battles with trucks aiming to kill or confrontations between a young boy and a vampire are indicative of deep-rooted problems or anxieties within the child.

While this is seldom the case, parents nevertheless tend to do one of two things in response to these fantastic or strange dreams. Due to their inability to understand the dream, parents generally ignore or dismiss the dream not knowing what to say; or, fearing the dream is the result of a particular problem the child has, they worry about the dream and what it may mean. An even greater concern to parents is that prolonged bad dreams or nightmares may be an indication of emotional problems. Again, the parents are at a loss as to how to handle the situation.

In the following pages, this book will address such issues and concerns facing parents and attempt to give them and other concerned adults a greater knowledge of the oftentimes wondrous, sometimes frightening world of children's dreams: what a dream is; what children tend to dream about; and how they can learn to communicate together with their child to better understand the meaning of their child's dreams. Knowing more about children's dreams will help adults identify what events are important to the child and how the child tends to deal with these important events.

Children's dreams often represent aspects of growing up in a confusing, less than obvious manner. By better understanding the important aspects of growing up and how they are revealed through dreams, parents can learn more about what matters most to their children, how to approach these issues, and how they can help their child along with the growing-up process.

In addition, a parent can learn a great deal about stress- and conflict-producing issues in their child's life. Inevitable and routine yet at times stressful events—such as separation and independence from parents, sibling rivalry, and peer relationships—are often represented in the themes of children's dreams. Likewise, more specific stress-related issues experienced by a child, such as a divorce between parents, the death of a parent, or a move to a new neighborhood, also can be better understood through the child's dreams.

This guide will continue with Chapter 16 by addressing the phenomenon of sleep and its physical components. Learning about when children begin to dream and when they distinguish dreaming from fantasy or daydreaming will also be discussed. Chapter 17 will attempt to help the parent understand the meaning of the child's dream content. Some pertinent historical viewpoints on the meaning of dreams as well as the results of contemporary research also will be reviewed. This chapter will attempt to give the reader a better understanding of children's dreams according to age and developmental differences.

Chapter 18 will deal with the frequent concerns of parents regarding nightmares. This chapter works toward a better understanding by parents of the most frightening and terrifying qualities of dreaming. A discussion of what parents can do to comfort their child in such instances is included. Finally, Chapter 19 will explore some techniques and suggestions for parents and other concerned individuals to help remember dreams and communicate their meaning between parent and child.

It is important to keep in mind that the purpose of

this guide is to give parents a better understanding of their child's dreams, thereby facilitating open communication between parent and child regarding important and at times stressful events in the child's life. The purpose is not to enable parents to psychoanalyze their child. The parent who, by learning more about the meaning of children's dream content, hopes to discover his or her child's reaction to the news that he or she will have to wait until birthday time for a new bike, or to understand the child's feelings about the parents' divorce, will be disappointed. Dreams are not that precise. However, used constructively, a better understanding of children's dreams can benefit both the parent and child by allowing them to better cope with stressful and routine circumstances that occur in daily life and are most important and meaningful to children.

Chapter 15

What Are Dreams?

LEARNING ABOUT SLEEP

In order to begin understanding dreams, we must first understand something about the process of sleep. Until approximately 50 years ago, scientists knew very little about sleep. Sleep was thought to be a passive and simple process during which the body "turned off" and was at rest.

As a result of the technological advances made within recent years, we now are able to know much more about sleep and its physical effects upon the body. As we fall asleep, our brain slows down but is still active and goes through certain cycles of rhythms that require about 24 hours to complete; this is why we sleep best at certain times of the day, poorly at others. When people are placed

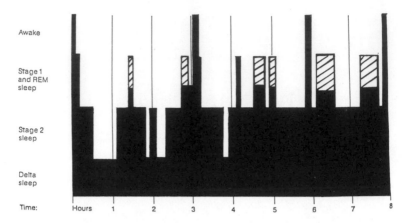

Figure 5. Stage 1 sleep and REM sleep (diagonals) are graphed on the same level because their EEG patterns are very similar.

in an environment without a clock but with plenty of food and light, they tend to maintain a basic cycle of sleep similar to that of their usual environment. Our body temperature lowers during sleep, rises throughout morning, and peaks with our own peak of activity or maximum energy efficiency. Our bodies cooperate with our physical and social needs of the day and night, and sleep is the means by which our body restores its energy and prepares for the next day.

Sleep researchers have broken sleep down into various stages. The stages are shown in Figure 5 and are identified by the brain waves produced during each stage. The brain waves we produce are measured by the EEG (electroencephalograph) and are generally believed to represent four stages of sleep. Stage one is considered the lightest stage of sleep and is a transitional period between wakefulness and sleep. In most sleepers, stage one generally lasts from a few seconds to a few minutes. It is during this time that we feel as if we are "drifting off" into sleep. While in this stage, we feel drowsy and can briefly maintain some connection or awareness of our room or surroundings, and we may think we are wide awake. We are, however, actually able to remember things around us with decreasing reliability, and we begin to lower consciousness and then fall quickly into a deeper stage of sleep.

Stage two is considered the first true stage of sleep, and often lasts approximately a few minutes to about half an hour. After that point, we then enter into stages three and four, the deepest stages of sleep referred to as delta sleep, a name once again reflective of the type of brain waves produced at this time. Stages one through four are considered NREM (pronounced non-REM) stages of sleep.

DREAMING

The dreaming cycles or stages are given the name REM (Rapid Eye Movement) sleep because of some of the physical characteristics of this stage of sleep. While most dreams are thought to occur during REM sleep, some dreams or parts of dreams are reported in NREM sleep as well. The first REM period of the night begins 60 minutes after sleep begins for children and about 90 minutes for adults. It usually lasts about five minutes; this is when the first dreaming state is likely to begin, at least for adults (some researchers believe young children do not have this particular stage of sleep). The next REM period of sleep occurs about 90 minutes later (three hours after the start of sleep) and lasts approximately 10 minutes. As this REM period reoccurs throughout the night, it will last approximately 10 minutes. We generally alternate every 90 minutes with a brief (15 minutes up to one hour) period of dreaming. Approximately four or five of these dreaming stages occur throughout the course of one night.

The sleep cycle for most children and adults is very regular and consistent. The cycles of sleep (REM or Stage One) occur every 90 minutes during the night. The first one tends to be the shortest, lasting less than 10 minutes; the later ones may last as long as 40 minutes to one hour. Most of this dreaming sleep occurs during the last third of the night, during the early morning hours of 4:00 A.M. through 7:00 A.M. for the average 11:00 P.M. to 7:00 A.M. sleeper. Our sleep is actually heaviest or deepest (as evidenced by brain wave patterns) during the first third of the night, from 11:30 P.M. to 3:00 A.M. for the average sleeper. Now that we have some technical information on sleep, let's return to more information on dreams themselves: when they begin for children, and how to identify them from fantasy and daydreams.

WHEN DO DREAMS BEGIN?

Infants spend an unusually large amount of time in REM sleep, often up to 80% of the total of all sleep for some premature infants. We are unable to know with any certainty when children begin to dream. Most researchers believe that children begin to dream sometime in their first year of life. When we observe sleeping infants, we can see that at certain times they toss and turn and cry or moan for a brief period; we know that this is not caused by hunger or any physical distress. Furthermore, a calm, reassuring pat on the back is often sufficient to comfort the infant. Such behavior is another indication of dreaming by the sleeping infant, yet this is knowledge locked within the child and his/her dreams.

DISTINGUISHING DREAMS FROM FANTASY
AND DAYDREAMS

As language begins to develop throughout the second year of life, however, we realize for sure that children do dream, yet another question then comes into consideration with young children: how can we tell dreams from fantasy, daydreaming, play, wishes, or real events? A child's ability to tell the difference between dreams and fantasy, imaginary play, or real events is influenced by many factors but is generally thought to occur between the ages of four and five.

The famous Swiss psychologist Jean Piaget (1929) described three stages in children's understanding of their dreams. During the first stage, occurring when the child is about five or six, the child experiences the dream as being outside of him- or herself. It is as if the dream were a play or movie taking place in front of the child and having nothing to do with him or her. During the second stage, which takes place when the child is about seven or eight, the dream begins to feel to the child as if it has something to do with his or her thoughts or ideas, but still takes on the appearance of occurring within the bedroom or "in front of his head" as one child described. Finally, during the third stage, at about ages eight or nine, the child experiences the dream as occurring within him- or herself, part of his or her own feelings, thoughts, and ideas. Yet, as previously noted, children can effectively begin to tell parents and others about their dreams and know the differences between dreams and other forms of fantasy beginning at about the ages of four or five.

Chapter 16

What Do Dreams Mean?

The topic of what children dream about is intriguing to almost anyone with even a passing interest in how the mind works or a fascination with dreams. Up until very recently, parents, educators, and psychologists alike were used to hearing only about those terrifying dreams in which children were awakened in fright in the middle of the night; or they heard about those dreams that survived in memory through the long night and were recalled the next morning. In fact, we now know that these dreams are only a very small portion of all the dreams children have during the course of a night's sleep.

To begin with, our scientific knowledge in this area derives from the study of physicians and psychologists in sleep laboratories. These are labs which are set up at hospitals and medical schools to learn more about the sleep and dream patterns of children and adults.

David Foulkes, a psychologist interested in this subject, decided to study children's dreams over a 5-year period in order to find out just what children do dream at different ages. His research, conducted at the University of Wyoming, studies the dreams of children who agreed (along with their parents) to sleep in the sleep laboratories and be awakened during their dream (REM) stages of sleep. The children were then asked to report on what they were dreaming at the time. The responses were scientifically studied and measured over the years, and the results were compiled, along with the many contributions from others who have studied children's dreams. The results provide some interesting and fascinating information.

WHAT CHILDREN'S DREAMS MEAN

Children dream every night and have at least three or four dreams nightly. Children usually dream about what is most important to them. The important events of the day—such as meeting a new friend, going to school, or breaking a favorite toy—will often make its appearance in the child's dreams. Likewise, the important people in a child's life, such as immediate family members and perhaps a close friend or two (particularly for the older school-aged child), will often be included in the dream. Some dreams reveal how children dream about the important events in their lives, such as winning a race or going on vacation. Children will dream about these meaningful situations, whether they are good or bad, happy or sad.

Sometimes parents become worried or concerned when important events that may be troubling the child turn up in his or her dreams. As parents know all too well, not every experience a child encounters is a happy or pleasant one. The death of a loved one, divorce, illness, a lost pet, and other disappointments and frustrations occur in children's lives, despite parents' wishes to prevent these events from ever happening. While we don't like to see our children experience sadness or pain, we realize at times they must. We also learn that with the support and guidance of parents, children do learn to cope and accept such events as part of life. Often such an event or one almost identical to it may occur and be reported in a child's dream. Many parents fear that their child is troubled and may be suffering emotionally when these events are relived or represented in the child's dreams. It is important to realize that dreams are a child's way of thinking at night. We know the brain doesn't go to sleep, just as the heart doesn't stop beating at night. If something important happens, it's quite natural for a child to think about it both day and night for quite a while. Thus, any significant or emotional event or the feelings connected with what happened are likely to make their appearance in the child's dreams, perhaps for some time to come, particularly if the situation is very important. Children have a remarkable opportunity to learn and develop the ability to cope with difficult events and circumstances in their dreams. In fact, dreaming can actually improve a child's capacity for adapting to significant events in his or her life as well as for learning new ways to adjust.

DEVELOPMENTAL ISSUES

Dreaming about a recent event is not an accident and does not occur by chance; besides reflecting the important occurrences of the day, dreams also tend to reflect the important emotional developments of a child at a particular age. For preschool aged children of four, five, or six, the major emotional objective is to begin to develop a sense of themselves as separate and independent. When children of this age play with friends, attend nursery school, or go to a play group for a few hours, they are in many ways beginning to prepare for the task of separating from their parents. This is a gradual process in which the child begins to take the necessary small steps to establish the security and confidence in themselves to play, learn, and meet others without the need to rush back to mother for comfort and security. These early social engagements are often of short duration and require the security of warm, loving parents awaiting the child's return home to serve the purpose of "emotional refueling." This provides the child with the self-security to take the necessary risks to meet and play with others. These are important issues, not to be taken lightly, particularly from the point of view of the preschooler. It is why, at times, sudden fears of leaving parents "come back" or uncertainty about that new dance class or birthday party unexpectedly appears.

Another important step in development for preschoolers is one that is referred to as sexual or gender identification. What is meant by identification is that process by which young boys or girls learn to see themselves as young boys or girls. It is a stage of development first ushered in by the three- or four-year-old girls who want to dress or be just like their moms or the young boys who must try to act just like their dads and carry a briefcase or tools. The child of this age wants to clearly establish a sense of self-identity for all to know. And the dreams of each tend to represent and reinforce this identification.

DIFFERENT DREAMS AT DIFFERENT AGES

Dreams of the Preschooler

Children also dream according to their ages and level of development. For the preschool-aged child, dreams usually include parents and may occasionally include a brother or sister. Inanimate objects like food, toys, or common objects like household furniture, utensils, or clothing frequently are important elements in a young child's life and are vividly incorporated into his or her dreams. The singing and dancing tree, the talking bird, or the laughing cookie are a blending of the normal and healthy life, and it is to be expected that these objects would be regularly part of the young child's dreams. Animals are frequently described in the dreams of preschool-aged children. Their frequent use in childhood story-telling and popular childhood entertainment—just think of Disney or Sesame Street characters—makes them a likely object of children's dreams. Some traditional psychological theories suggest they may represent some of the basic needs of children, although their frequent use and easy identification in our popular culture is a liklier explanation. Usually the content of the dream is unclear, sometimes confusing, to an adult perhaps even bizarre. A dream by one such preschooler is a case in point:

> Steve told of a dream he had recently when he was out trick-or-treating. He came up to a big house and stopped to look inside a window. When he looked into the window, a big, mechanical screwdriver kept coming closer and closer towards him. It came right up to him and wrenched his nose. Steve was so scared the dream woke him up.

Steve's dream not only incorporates a recent event like Halloween (the dream was reported a few days after Halloween), but it also includes the strange fantasy-like events so typical of young children's dreams. Steve's dream, on the surface, is an example of a young boy who isn't quite sure if it is all right to explore the world around him. When he dares to do so he is in danger, a situation typical of the psychological task of separating and establishing some emotional independence. As one of the important developmental tasks of the preschool child, such events are often represented in dream content.

Dreams of the Early School-Aged Child

The dreams of the early school-aged child also contain a curious mix of real and unreal, familiar and unfamiliar, bizarre and mundane. While lifelike inanimate objects are often seen in the dreams of early school-aged children, they are nevertheless less common than in dreams of the younger child. There is also a slight increase in the number of main characters represented in the dreams to include a few important friends or people besides family members. Representations of the budding sexual feelings in the dreams of children of this age are abundant. Perhaps one of the surprising aspects of this age of development is the fact that the early sexual feelings often begin at this time, although they are minimal and usually go unnoticed. While it's usually impossible and not important for parents to recognize such thoughts and feelings in the dreams of their child, it does help to be aware that such thoughts do exist, and an opportunity to discuss them (such feelings) with a child may present itself when talking about dreams or other matters.

Authority figures usually play an important part in

the life of a young school-aged child. The child is expanding, usually for the first time, his or her social world to
include school, clubs or activities, parents of their friends,
and the environment as a whole. These new experiences
increase the child's contact with other adults like teachers, store managers, policemen, bus drivers, parents of
friends. These activities bring the child into contact with
other adults of authority. The process of doing so enables
the child to question, for the very first time, the views of
parents and to begin to question the validity of the opinions and knowledge of people other than mom and dad.
These authority figures are often represented in dreams
by fantasy figures such as kings and queens or more contemporary figures such the characters in *Star Wars* or
popular television shows.

Many parents are concerned with expressions of
aggression or anger in thought, action, or dreams. Yet,
the child of this age will naturally have dreams full of
scary, threatening creatures borrowed from movies, television, literature, or the direct products of his or her
imagination. Often times, these dreams are told with obvious excitement and energy by the child. At the same
time, parents may also be concerned with some unre-
leased hostile emotions they feel the child needs to express. While such expression is usually helpful for the
child, it is not always possible or necessary to put the
feelings into words. Dreams accomplish part of this task
and serve by themselves as a normal expression of
thoughts and feelings, including angry ones if necessary.
The themes and events of such dreams can frighten parents because of their hostility and aggression but they need
not worry. Simply by talking about the dream itself without ever mentioning any actual event it may obviously
represent in the child's real world, parents can discover

what a child is thinking, his views and reactions, and possible ways of dealing with these issues.

Children of early school age are primarily occupied by their newfound involvement with a rapidly expanding social world. Suddenly, friendships with many children, not just the select few of a neighborhood or day-care center, are thrust upon the child. These new social relationships also tend to lessen the child's emotional dependence upon parents. The ever solidifying gender or sexual identity occurring is reinforced by a retreat into the safety of a same-sex play group. It is a time when the "no girls allowed" sign is prominently displayed on the clubhouse door and girls want absolutely nothing to do with the boys on the playground. As every parent of an older child knows, these attitudes are quite brief and seem to change soon enough. The dreams of children at this time are likely to reflect these social dilemmas and changing views.

Chapter 17

What about Nightmares?

Few things are as terrifying to parents as to hear their child awaken screaming and crying about a nightmare. They rush into the bedroom to comfort and console their sobbing, sometimes panic-stricken child, wondering what caused this abrupt disruption of sleep. More often than not, the child is easily consoled and returns to sleep without difficulty. It is often the child's parents, however, who then have difficulty returning to sleep, lying awake full of questions. What was that nightmare about and what did it mean? Is my child troubled or worried about something? What about the frequent or recurring nightmare, when will that stop? These and other similar questions are frequently asked by parents and at times even by the child because nightmares raise many questions as to their meaning and cause.

WHAT DO NIGHTMARES MEAN?

First we need to begin with the definition of a nightmare. Webster's defines a nightmare as follows: "Formerly, an evil spirit that was believed to haunt and suffocate sleeping people"; secondly, "A frightening dream, often accompanied by a sensation of helplessness and hopelessness." Aside from primitive cultures and beliefs, nightmares are not considered evil spirits but are frightening dreams accompanied by feelings of panic and stress as well as oppression and helplessness. A well-accepted general (nontechnical) definition of a nightmare is: waking up from sleep with a terrified feeling or waking up from a dream with frightened feelings (the cause of awakening was not external). Depending on the age of the dreamers and their ability to verbally express what they remember, nightmares are characterized by terrifying figures such as monsters or frightening people who are trying to scare the dreaming child. Usually the dreamer can remember who was in the dream and what happened in the dream, often with much detail. Nightmares tend to become more and more complicated and detailed the longer they continue before waking occurs. The younger the child, the less he or she are able to remember and report about their nightmare. Parents should not expect young children under the ages of six or eight to report with any clarity or certainty what they recall from a nightmare. Occasionally, some elements such as who or what was chasing them, how they were in danger, or how they escaped is recalled. Many but not all dreamers, regardless of age, survive the threat or danger and "make it through" the peril they experience in their dreams. Usually the dreamer is awakened prior to a catastrophe or death. During a long seemingly endless fall from a cliff the dreamer will usually awaken just before he or she is hurt, injured, or killed. Likewise, the threatened child will usually manage to escape from whoever or whatever is chasing him or her. While this is not always the case, it appears to be the rule, although this fact is less true in the dream reports of emotionally disturbed children and adolescents. More about this fact will be described in Chapter 19. Generally, an adaptive quality or survival instinct functions or is operative in our dream world as in waking reality. These psychological processes are considered to be important factors that frequently keep us alive or constantly escaping danger or death in our dreams.

WHY DO CHILDREN HAVE NIGHTMARES?

When do nightmares begin and who has them? The research findings on sleep and dreaming are imprecise and, while it is improving all the time, it remains difficult to know for sure about the accuracy of information we have on dreams. Dreams are difficult to remember and even more difficult to study.

Most scientists and researchers suggest that the chance of nightmares occurring as early as dreaming does is quite likely. Thus, nightmares may occur as early as the first year of life. As we discussed earlier, the preverbal child and the preschool age child have great difficulty distinguishing dreaming from fantasy or reality. Much of what parents report as "waking up crying," a sleepless night, or even colic are perhaps nightmares experienced by an infant or toddler. The studies conducted appear to suggest that the likelihood of nightmares is greatest for the child under the ages of five or six. The number of those preschool children who have nightmares regularly (once a week or more) seems to vary from 5% to 10% for children seven years and under. The numbers steadily decrease throughout childhood although some reports indicate a brief and slight increase in nightmares during adolescence, normally a time of stress and anxiety. Many studies then show that the rate of those who report nightmares decreases to about 5% for adults. Although the figures are consistent, we do not fully understand why this is so.

Males and females seem to have an equal number of nightmares, although the rate of nightmares reported is greater for adult females. This is attributed largely to the fact that women seem more able to report or "admit" to having a nightmare than men. In our culture, men or older boys may consider themselves less manly if they admit to being frightened by a dream.

Medical illness and social stress may increase the number of nightmares experienced by adults and children. Emotional problems or worries also seem to cause a change in the types of dreams children have and produce a greater number of nightmares.

Studies with adults suggest that those who frequently experience nightmares (more than one per week) still represent a small percentage (5%) of the population. These people can generally be described as sensitive adults who tend to be vulnerable and open to their own feelings as well as to those of others. These individuals tend to have definite artistic and creative tendencies and skills. In many ways, those who have difficulty holding back or repressing these intense, painful thoughts or feelings tend to have more nightmares. There is no skill or practice to avoid having nightmares and no reason to do so for that matter. While upsetting and disrupting to the dreamer's sleep and the sleep of others, nightmares are only dreams and should not be cause for fear or worry to children or their parents. The previously described, more terrifying night terrors are clearly distinguishable from nightmares. Generally, they can be corrected easily with a brief course of medication after proper identification and consultation from a physician.

NIGHT TERRORS

There is a very specific biological and psychological occurrence commonly mistaken for a nightmare; it is called a night terror. This disturbance is identified primarily by the abrupt arousal from sleep, usually early in the night, characterized by screaming and thrashing about with rapid changes in heart rate, the nervous system, and little recall of any dream. In fact, night terrors are believed by many to be disturbances of arousal or awakening and not the results of dreaming or nightmares. Most reports of nightmares by adults and children (when verbally able) include a long memory of the dream leading up to the nightmare itself. Night terrors are puzzling in that the dreamer does not remember or believe his terror to be a dream but rather a sudden, unexpected, terrorized feeling with little memory of any dream associated with it. Night terrors need to be identified as distinct from nightmares; while less likely to occur, they can be treated successfully.

Chapter 18

Techniques for Parents

It is important to remember that understanding dreams and their meaning is an active ongoing process between parent (or other adult) and child. The key to remember is that this process is an active interchange between parent and child in which the child is encouraged to participate and exchange thoughts, memories, and ideas about dreams with a caring, interested adult.

Children not only welcome the interest and excitement of a parent or of a caring adult in their lives, they cherish and require it. A child's sense of self-esteem and identity is formulated in part upon the sense of self-worth, praise, and encouragement that the significant adults in his life impart to the child. The eagerly excited pre-schooler wants nothing more than to proudly display his drawings, recite the alphabet, or exhibit his speed in a race to an appreciative parent. Similarly, the school-aged child is thrilled to bring home a good report card or impress dad with the ability to hammer a nail or bake cupcakes "as good as mom's." The reward gained is the sense of accomplishment encouraged by the parents. The benefits of a job well done are lost and practically nonexistent for a young child without the encouragement, support, and appreciation of the parents or other important adults in his or her life.

TECHNIQUES TO IMPROVE DREAM RECALL

The same interest in and appreciation of the dreams of children by their parents produce a similar sense of inner security. Dreams become important, meaningful, and worth recalling. If parents show an interest and excitement in what their children dream, children will be better able to remember their dreams, will display a greater interest and appreciation for their meaning, and will be more interested in discussing their dreams.

As indicated earlier, our ability to remember is diminished during sleep, thus reducing our (adult or child's) capacity to remember what we dreamed. Typically, the frightening or terrifying dream startles the dreamers so that they often awake (at least briefly); the dream is so vivid that more of it is incorporated into memory than would otherwise be the case. We also know that we dream more than we recall. Research on dreams indicates that children who are encouraged to remember their dreams and describe what they do remember show an increasing capacity to remember more and more about their dreams as time goes on. Likewise, children who have or are encouraged to express themselves artistically (through drawings, artwork, dance) reveal an increased ability to remember their dreams as well. The results of a number of research efforts indicate that intelligence or economic/ social status of a child or his family has little to do with the ability to recall dreams or affect the meaning of these dreams. The meaning of this information can be used to suggest a practical application for parents and their children regarding recalling dreams and understanding their meaning: practice makes perfect. The more they are asked to remember or talk about their dreams, the better they are able to remember.

There are some easy methods for parents to use to help their children remember their dreams. Research has proven that the closer we awaken a dreaming child to the time they are dreaming, the more they can remember about their dreams. We do not suggest that parents stay up all night next to their sleeping children and awaken them when they suspect they are dreaming. The technique we used to help children remember dreams is simple and effective. Children place some paper and a pen or pencil next to their bed at night and write and/or draw something about their dream or dreams as soon as they wake up. We then meet with the children as early as possible the next morning to discuss the dreams. They can use their notes and/or drawings to help them remember what they dreamed. This technique is not generally usable with much success for children under the age of six, but of course it can be tried. Parents can use the same method at home. Children are often very eager to try something new, particularly if it is presented to them as "a game" and/or is of interest and excitement to their parents.

Younger children can be asked directly what they remember about their dreams of the preceding night. The responses are often genuine and to the point. It is important to remember that children (and adults for that matter) often do not remember their dreams, something particularly true with young children or when first beginning to discuss a child's dreams. The ability to remember dreams generally improves over time as the child becomes more interested in remembering dreams and talking about them. Parents who are interested in hearing their child's dreams and who ask about them will stimulate the child's interest and ability to remember dreams. Parents should also note that the length of dreams remembered can be and often is quite short for young children. One, two, or three sentences are more typical of the length of children's dreams than longer, detailed narratives. As a child's intellectual and verbal skills develop, the length and detail of dreams expand.

A comment or two about making up dreams may be helpful at this point. Children, particularly younger children, will often make up a dream in order to please a curious adult who is at the edge of his seat, anxiously awaiting the first syllables of recollection offered by a young dreamer. For the purpose of encouraging, remembering, and discussing dreams, made-up dreams are fine. They should not be discouraged, for the child may feel he must "produce" dreams or he has failed. In this situation, the made-up dream can often contain some of the same elements of wishes, important events, and memories and thoughts about what is most important to the child at that time. Likewise, the practice of parent and child talking about these important thoughts and events improves the technique of verbally communicating such material between parent and child. The related benefits of making the child feel important and fulfilled—that his thoughts and ideas are interesting and important—can be achieved equally well through the made-up dream.

COMMUNICATING ABOUT DREAMS

Once the dream itself has been shared between parent and child, the next step is to help the child understand what the dream content or material may mean to him or her. An example of this method at work follows.

> One preschooler named Joey dreamed he was with his mother, father, and brothers, who went to the circus with him. At the circus, he saw a clown with big eyes and a bubble for a nose. Joey thought the clown was funny, but then he came up to Joey and popped a balloon in his face and scared him. For the rest of the show, the clown was bad and mean to everybody else but it was something he couldn't help.

Joey's dream may represent feelings of anger and frustration which he places or projects onto the clown rather than himself. This is quite a normal emotional experience for children and in various (more sophisticated) forms takes place throughout adulthood as well; it is a way of coping with feelings and behaviors unacceptable to one's own self-image. Joey probably felt he too was "bad and mean" as the clown was, "but it was something he couldn't help." One might speculate that Joey had done something (perhaps to one of his brothers) that was intended to be funny but was not received that way; that behavior may have led to a squabble or disagreement between himself and his brothers or his parents. Of course, such behaviors are typical for preschool-aged children and fit into normal development patterns, as does Joey's way of dealing with the issues in his dream.

In order to try to elicit the meaning of the child's dream content, the best approach is to simply ask the child, "What do you think that means?" A first common response may be to repeat or state the obvious. In our example, Joey might say: "I don't like balloons being popped in my face." If no other comments or ideas follow, the adult may ask the child a clarifying question or two regarding the possible underlying or latent content. This might include a question about the clown and why he was bad and mean to everybody else and why it was something he couldn't help or why he popped the balloon in Joey's face. It is very important the adult listen very carefully to what the child says in response. Those comments are likely to contain the key elements of the dream to the child.

The story of interaction in the dream itself is what is called the manifest content. This material is important and tells us much about what thoughts, feelings, and behaviors are important to the child. Responses to any of the clarifying questions also reveal how a child adapts to certain situations important to him or her. These insights reveal much about what a child may be thinking and dealing with emotionally in his or her life at that time and are also indicative of the child's means of coping with or adapting to those issues.

Finally, the material discussed and learned also can provide an opportunity to identify and approach an issue directly (or consciously) on a child's mind. The example of a dream of an eight-year-old boy that follows will help illustrate his point:

> Carl told of a dream that happened one night, after he and his little brother got into an argument earlier that same day. Carl dreamed about how mad he still was at his little brother. In his dream, he got so mad about who would play with their favorite truck that he hit his brother. He was dreaming that he had all the toys he wanted to play with all by himself when,

all of a sudden, he heard a noise from far far away. The noise got louder and louder, and kept getting closer and closer. Then a great big bulldozer appeared. Carl had never seen one so big before; it was bigger than his whole house! It kept getting closer and closer and closer. It was coming after him! Carl was very scared. He started to run and run, all the way into his house. The great big bulldozer was right behind. He got into his house just in time, and he was now safe from the giant bulldozer.

Carl not only is dreaming about some likely guilt over hitting his brother, but he may also be describing his father's reaction through that of the bulldozer. Children often have very symbolic representations of those important to them. To many little boys, their dads are represented in symbolic images; by a king, a lion or, in this case, a bulldozer.

Clarifying questions can add much to what has already been learned from the manifest content of a dream. If Carl were able to describe how he felt about hitting his little brother or more about where the bulldozer came from, we might learn more about his feelings of sibling rivalry, anger, guilt, or parental limit-setting. The adult can ask the child if a situation (manifest dream content) has ever happened or if he or she ever experienced the thoughts about what it means to them (latent content). This allows the child to make a direct connection to what he or she thinks about the dream and him- or herself. By first reviewing this process as it pertains to somebody else in a dream, it lessens any emotionally charged response and places it onto somebody or something else. This is a technique used frequently in play therapy by clinicians to elicit a child's feelings and can be effectively modified in discussion about dreams for the same purpose.

The overall benefit of such communication cannot be underestimated. Any opportunity to discuss important events and to learn about a child's adaptive responses and emotional reactions to situations is always helpful. This process aids the child in thinking about such events and allows the parent to take part in helping the child understand and address the issues involved in growing up.

Appendixes

APPENDIX A. ERIKSON'S EIGHT STAGES OF PSYCHOSOCIAL DEVELOPMENT

Stage I	Basic trust versus mistrust
Stage II	Autonomy versus shame and doubt
Stage III	Initiative versus guilt
Stage IV	Industry versus inferiority
Stage V	Identity versus role diffusion
Stage VI	Intimacy versus isolation
Stage VII	Generativity versus stagnation
Stage VIII	Ego integrity versus despair

APPENDIX B. DREAM SCORES DERIVED FROM THE ELKAN CHECKLIST BY AGE

Developmental crisis level	Age groups		
	4–5	8–9	14–15
I–III	19	7	3
IV	1	12	3
V–VIII	0	1	14

APPENDIX C. MACK'S DREAM SCORES OF NORMAL AND DISTURBED 14–15-YEAR-OLD BOYS

Groups	Crisis level							
	I	II	III	IV	V	VI	VII	VIII
14–15-year-old "normal" boys	1		4	6	5			
14–15-year-old disturbed boys	1	1	8	4	1			

APPENDIX D. CATEGORIES OF DISTURBED
ADOLESCENTS USED IN THIS STUDY

Category I: Ed-severe

- Bizarre delusions, including thoughts of being controlled, somatic, grandiose, persecutory or nihilistic delusions
- Auditory hallucinations
- Incoherence or loose associations, markedly illogical thinking
- Catatonic or disorganized behavior
- Distinct periods of significantly elevated or irritable moods
- Dysphoric mood with loss of interest in usual activities; marked by symptoms of sad, hopeless, depressed mood
- The continued presence of: poor appetite or weight loss; sleep disturbance; psychomotor retardation or disturbance; decreased interest in usual activities; loss of energy; difficulty with concentration; recurring thoughts of death or suicide.

Category II: Ed-moderate

- Frequent panic attacks
- Episodic and recurring fear of being alone in public places
- Persistent and irrational fears to avoid humiliation and embarrassment
- Persistent anxiety with: motor tension, autonomic hyperactivity, apprehension, and restlessness or irritability
- Obsessions: recurrent, persistent thoughts, ideas, images, or impulses that are ego-dystonic

- Compulsions: repetitive and purposeful behaviors performed in ritualistic fashion
- Reexperienced trauma
- Repetitive and persistent aggression toward others which may include: physical violence, lack of empathy with or without violation of the rights of others
- Unrealistic future worries with somatic complaints, excessive concern and anxiety
- Isolation, avoidance, and lack of interest in any social contacts or severe distress regarding identity
- Eating disorders with disturbance of body image

Category III: Ed-mild

- Difficulty in reaction to identifiable stressors which may include disturbance of: mood, emotions, conduct, academies (or work), or any combination of the above
- Phase of life—situational or developmental stressors which produce complications not significant enough to warrant another diagnosis; these may include academic or work problems, bereavement, divorce or marriage-related family problems, financial stress

APPENDIX E. COVER LETTER FOR
TREATMENT PROVIDERS

Dear ———:

This letter is to confirm my visit with the Adolescent Unit Directors. I have enclosed a copy of my research design as well as a copy of a recent article, which describes some relevant background as to my view of the meaning and use of dream content in treatment with children.

Briefly stated, I believe that dream content represents a combination of symbolic representations of developmental norms, selective recall of important events preceding the dream, and wish fulfillment. For a variety of reasons, we can recall only a small portion of our entire dream content and usually only a select few (often the most affective in content or in our response) end up in treatment discussions.

My research is an effort to learn more about the dream content of adolescents with emotional disturbances as compared with a control group of "normal" adolescents. Secondly, I hope to try and establish a link between developmental theory and dream content by testing a hypothesis that tests whether adolescents with "more severe" emotional disturbances (e.g., schizophrenic and affective disorders) will reveal dream content which developmentally is indicative of greater fixation or regression than those adolescents with "mild" emotional disturbances (e.g., adjustment disorders). If correct, the implications can assist in the diagnostic and treatment indicators of assessing the developmental functioning of our clients as well as in providing another means of learning more and communicating about the issues of greatest importance.

I hope this brief discussion is helpful. The enclosed proposal and my discussion will describe the methodology for collecting the dream content from your patients in detail. Please call if you have any questions. I look forward to seeing you soon.

APPENDIX F. CONSENT LETTER
FOR PARENTS

Dear Parent:

I am conducting a study to help therapists and counselors better understand the meaning of children's dreams. The goal of this research is to help understand the meaning of dreams among adolescents.

The study is simple and will take only a little time. If you and your son/daughter agree to participate, I will ask them to place some paper next to the bed at night and to write and/or draw something the next morning to help them remember their dream(s) from the night before. Later that day, I will meet with him or her and ask what their dreams were.

You and your child's privacy will be respected. No names or information will be identified in the results. The research will comply with all the professional standards and ethical considerations for conducting research which emphasizes confidentiality and safety. If you have any questions about the research or the procedure, please feel free to contact me.

If you and your child are willing to participate in this study, please sign the enclosed form and return it to me in the enclosed stamped envelope. I will be in touch with you soon to ask you to fill out a brief questionnaire. Thank you very much for your time and interest and I hope you can help me in this study.

APPENDIX G. CONSENT FORM

I ___parent's name___ agree to allow my son or daughter to participate in the research being conducted by Mr. Catalano. I understand that the study will comply with all professional standards for conducting such research, which emphasize privacy of the material and the assurance of no risk to those participating.

_____

parent's signature

_____

date

APPENDIX H. DATA ANALYSIS DESIGN

1. Determining sample size:

A. Statistics used: *T* test; one way analysis of variance.

B. Power analysis: A difference of .7 has been determined to be a minimally important effect size. This has been determined using the sample size of Mack's (1974) study; the level of significance (L.O.S.) and the statistics used; *t* test and one way analysis of variance.

C. Alpha risk: $\alpha = .05$
Beta risks: $\beta = .20$
Power analysis: $= .80$

D. An *n* of 27 for each group—1. emotionally disturbed and 2. "normal" adolescents—has been determined using the Cohen Tables for sample size (Cohen, 1977, pp. 30-31).

E. A sample size of 27 for each independent sample $(U_{ed}$ and $U_n)$ will be used. An attempt to evenly distribute the group of emotionally disturbed adolescents (U_{ed}) will also be made (see below):

$$U_{ed} = 27 \qquad U_{ed} = se = 7$$
$$U_{ed} = mo = 12$$
$$U_n = 27 \qquad U_{ed} = mi = 8$$

2.   Descriptive diagrams of the ex post facto research for hypothesis I:

   Population 1: Emotionally disturbed adolescents:

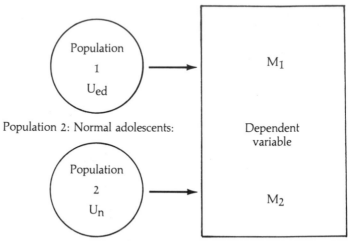

   Population 2: Normal adolescents:

   Dependent variable: The developmental
   level reflected in dream content.

3. Test of the hypotheses; a proposed *t* test for the hypotheses:
   A.   Ha: $U_{ed} < U_n$
         Ho: $U_{ed} < U_n$

   B.   A *t* test for independent samples: $U_{ed} = U_n = 27$

   C.   .05 level of significance, one tailed:
         df = 50
         + ≤ 1.678

D. Descriptive diagram for hypothesis II: The diagram below
    illustrates the research design:

Dependent variable:

Population

1

$U_{ed} = se$

$U_{ed} = se$ = most severe emotional
                disorders

M_1

Population

2

$U_{ed} = mo$

$U_{ed} = mo$ = moderately severe

M_2

Population

3

$U_{ed} = mi$

$U_{ed} = mi$ = least severe

M_3

Population

4

U_n

U_n = normal

M_4

Dependent variable = the developmental level
reflected in the dream content

E.   Test of hypothesis II; a test for one-way analysis of
      variance:

      A.   Ha: U_{ed} = $_{se}$ = U_{ed} = $_{mo}$ = U_{ed} = $_{mi}$ < U_n

           Ho: U_{ed} = $_{se}$ = U_{ed} = $_{mo}$ = U_{ed} = $_{mi}$ = U_n

      B.   Simple analysis of variance

      C.   .05 level of significance, df = 3.48, F ≥ 2.84

APPENDIX I. DEFINITION OF TERMS

Developmental theory   A theoretical position incorporating the view that psychological growth is psychosocially oriented and is progressive and sequential in nature. Developmental theory suggests that specific stages of growth occur which incorporate intrapsychic and social tasks, conflicts and crises. Successful completion and mastery of each stage is considered essential to ensure continued growth and maturation in subsequent stages (see Chapter 2 for further detail).

Elkan checklist   A scoring instrument designed by Elkan (1969) to measure the developmental level reflected in manifest dream content. The checklist was formulated based upon Erikson's theory of psychosocial developmental stages (see Chapter 3 for further detail).

Highest developmental level scoring method   The scoring method originally designed by Elkan which scores the developmental level of a subject's dream content according to the highest level of developmental functioning reported in the dream (see Chapter 3 for further detail).

Latent dream content   The underlying meaning and associations of the content of the dream that are usually beyond the conscious awareness of the dreamer (see Chapter 2 for further detail).

Manifest dream content   The recall of the events, circumstances, and details of the dream as remembered and reported by the dreamer (see Chapter 2 for further detail).

Mean developmental level scoring method   An alternative scoring method which scores the developmental functioning of a subject's dream content according to the mean score of developmental functioning reported in the dream (see Chapter 4 for further detail).

Structured recall method of data collection   A method of data collection for dream content designed to stimulate interest, recall, and reporting of dreams (see Chapter 3 for further detail).

References

Ablon, S. L., & Mack, J. E. (1980). Children's dreams reconsidered. *The Psychoanalytical Study of the Child, 30,* 185.

Adler, A. (1958). *What life should mean to you.* Capricorn Press: New York. (Original work published in 1931)

American Psychiatric Association (1980). Diagnostic criteria. In *Diagnostic and Statistical Manual of Mental Disorders* (3rd ed.). Washington, D.C.: American Psychiatric Association.

Ammons, R., & Ammons, C. (1962). The quick test (QT) monograph supplement, i–vii *Psychological reports,* Southern Universities Press.

Aserinsky, E., & Kleitman, N. Regularly occurring periods of eye motility and concomitant phenomena during sleep. *Science, 118,* (1953) 273–274.

Beck, Henry W. (1977). Dream analysis in family therapy, *Clinical Social Work, 1,* 53–57.

Blanchard, P. (1926). A study of subject matter and motivation of children's dreams. *Journal of Abnormal and Social Pathology, 21,* 24–37.

Blanck, G., & Blanck, R. (1979). *Ego psychology II: Psychoanalytic developmental psychology.* New York: Columbia University Press.

211

Blos, P. (1967). The second individuation process of adolescence. In R. S. Eissler, (Eds.), *The Psychoanalytical Study of the Child* (Vol. 22, pp. 162–186). New York: International Universities Press.

Blos, P. (1962). *On Adolescence: A psychoanalytical interpretation.* New York: Free Press.

Bornstein, B. (1946). Hysterical twilight states in an eight-year-old child. *The Psychoanalytical Study of the Child, 2,* 229–240.

Brenner, C. (1974). *An elementary textbook of psychoanalysis.* New York: International Universities Press.

Bussell, J., Dement, W., & Pivik, T. (1972). *The eye movement-imagery relationship in REM sleep and waking.* Paper presented at New York.

Cason, H. (1935). The nightmare of dream. *Psychological Monographs, 461*(5).

Catalano, S. (1984). Children's dreams: Their meaning and use in clinical practice. *Child and Adolescent Social Work Journal, 1*(4), 280–289.

Cowger, C. D. (1984). Statistical significance tests: Scientific ritualism or scientific method? *Social Service Review, 4,* 363.

Edward, J. (1987). Dream analysis in family therapy. *Clinical Social Work, 1,* 53–57.

Edward J. (1987). The dream as a vehicle for the recovery of childhood trauma, *Clinical Social Work Journal, 15*(4), 356–360.

Elkan, B. (1969). *Developmental differences in the manifest content of children's reported dreams.* Unpublished doctoral dissertation, Columbia University.

Erikson, E. H. (1959). Identity and the life cycle. *Psychological Issues, 1,* 18–171.

Erikson, E. (1950). *Childhood and society* (2nd ed.). New York: W. W. Norton.

Erikson, E. (1953). Growth and crisis in the "healthy personality." In C. Kluckhohn & H. Murray (Eds.), *Personality in nature, society and culture* (2nd ed.). New York: Knopf Press, pp. 185–225.

Erikson, E. (1954). The dream specimen of psychoanalysis. In R. P. Knight & C. R. Friedman (Eds.), *Psychoanalytical psychiatry and psychology.* New York: International Universities Press, pp. 131–170.

Erikson, E. (1964). *Insight and personality.* New York: W. W. Norton.

Farnsworth, D. L. (1966). *Psychiatry, education and the young adult.* Springfield, Ill.: Charles C. Thomas.

Foster, J. C., & Anderson, J. E. (1936). Unpleasant dreams in childhood. *Child Development, 7,* 77–84.

Foulkes, D. (1962). Dream reports from different stages of sleep. *Journal of Abnormal Social Psychology, 65,* 16–25.

Foulkes, D. (1967). Dreams of the male child: Four case studies. *Journal of Child Psychology, 8,* 81–98.

Foulkes, D. (1967). Nonrapid eye movement. *Experimental Neurology,* (4), 28–38.

Foulkes, D. (1969). Drug research and the meaning of dreams. *Experimental Medical Surgery, 27,* 39–52.

Foulkes, D. (1970). Personality and dreams. In E. Hartmann (Ed.), *Sleep and Dreaming* (pp. 147–153). Boston: Little and Brown.

Foulkes, D. (1982). *Children's dreams: Longitudinal studies.* New York: John Wiley.

Foulkes, D., & Pivik, T. (1969). NREM mentation: Relation to personality, orientation time, and time of night. *Journal of Consulting Clinical Psychology, 32,* 144–151.

Foulkes, D., & Rechtschaffen, A. (1964). Presleep determinants of dream content: Effect of two films. *Perceptual and Motor Stresses, 19,* 983–1005.

Foulkes, D., Larson, J., Swanson, E., & Radin, M. (1969). Two studies of childhood dreaming. *American Journal of Orthopsychiatry, 39,* 627–643.

Foulkes, D., Pivik, T., Steadman, H., Spear, P., & Symonds, J. (1967). Dreams of the male child: An EEG study. *Journal of Abnormal Psychology, 72,* 457–467.

Fraiberg, S. (1959). *The magic years.* New York: Scribner's.

Fraiberg, S. (1965). A comparison of the analytical method in two stages of a child analysis. *Journal of the American Academy of Child Psychiatry, 4,* 387–400.

French, T., & Fromm, E. (1964). *Dream interpretation.* New York: Basic Books.

Freud, A. (1965). *Normality and pathology in childhood: Assessments of development.* New York: International Universities Press.

Freud, A. (1966). The ego and mechanisms of defense. In *The writings of Anna Freud,* Vol. 2. New York: International Universities Press. (Originally published in 1936)

Freud, S. (1953a). *The interpretation of dreams.* London: Hogarth Press. (Original work published 1900)

Freud, S. (1953b). *The introductory letters of psychoanalysis.* London: Hogarth Press.

Freud, S. (1959). Fragment of an analysis of a case of hysteria. *Collected papers* (pp. 106–113). New York: Basic Books.

Green, M. R. (1971). Clinical significance of children's dreams. In J. H. Massernon (Ed.), *Dream Dynamics* (pp. 72–97). New York: Grune and Stratton.

Greenberg, R., & Pearlman, C. (1975). A psychoanalytical dream continuum. *International Review of Psychoanalysis, 2,* 441–448.

Greenberg, R., & Pearlman, C. (1978). If Freud only knew. *International Review of Psychoanalysis, 5,* 71–75.

Group for the Advancement of Psychiatry. (1968). *Normal Adolescence Group for the Advancement of Psychiatry, 6*(68).

Hall, C. (1953). The cognitive theory of dreams. *Journal of General Psychology, 49,* 273–282.

Hall, C. & Van de Castle, R. (1966). *The content analysis of dreams.* New York: Appleton-Century Crofts.

Hartmann, H. (1939). *Ego psychology and the problem of adaptation.* New York: International Universities Press.

Hartmann, H. (1950). *Essays on ego psychology.* New York: International Universities Press.

Hartmann, H. (1964) *Essays on ego psychology.* New York: International Universities Press.

Hartmann, H., & Kris E. (1945). The genetic approach in psychoanalysis. *The Psychoanalytic Study of the Child, 2,* 11–38.

Hartmann, H., Kris, E. & Lowenstein, R. M. (1946). Comments on the formation of psychic structure. *The Psychoanalytic Study of the Child, 2,* 11–38.

Hartmann, H., Kris, E. & Lowenstein, R. M. (1949). Notes on the theory of aggression. *The Psychoanalytic Study of the Child. 3/4,* 9–36.

Hirschberg, J. C. (1966). Dreaming, drawing and the dream screen in the psychoanalysis of 1 2-1/2-year-old boy. *American Journal of Psychiatry, 122,* 37–45.

Hobson, J. A., & McCarley, R. W. (1984, August 27). Medical Research. *The Boston Globe,* p. 40.

Jacobson, E. (1964a). *The self and the object world.* New York: International Universities Press.

Jacobson, E. (1964b). *The affects and their pleasure-unpleasure qualities in relation to the psychic discharge process in drives, affects, behavior. 1,* 38–66.

Jesild, A. T., Markey, F. V., & Jersild, L. L. (1933). Children's fears, dreams, wishes, daydreams, likes, dislikes pleasant and unpleasant memories. *Child Development Monographs,* 12. Teachers College, Columbia University.

Jones, R. M. (1970). *The new psychology of dreaming*. New York: Grune and Stratton.

Josselyn, J. M. (1971). *Adolescence*. New York: Harper & Row.

Jung, C. G. (1972). General aspects of dream psychology. In *Dreams* (pp. 23–66). Princeton, N.J.: Princeton University Press. (Originally published in 1948)

Kernberg, O. (1976). *Object relations theory and clinical psychoanalysis*. New York: Jason Aronson.

Kernberg, O. (1980). *Internal world and external reality; Object relations theory applied*. New York: Jason Aronson.

Klein, M. (1932). *The psycho-analysis of children*. London: Hogarth Press.

Kohut, H. (1971). *The analysis of the self*. New York: International Universities Press.

Kohut, H. (1977). *The restoration of the self*. New York: International Universities Press.

Kris, E. (1950). Notes on the developmental and some current problems of psychoanalytical child psychology. *Psychoanalytical Study of the Child, 5*, 24–26.

Langs, R. J. (1967). Manifest dreams in adolescents: A controlled pilot study. *Journal of Nervous and Mental Diseases, 145*, 43–52.

Lewis, M. (1973). *Clinical aspects of child development: An introductory synthesis of psychological concepts and clinical problems*. Philadelphia: Lea and Febiger.

Lucente, L. (1987). The dream: Mechanisms and clinical applications. *Clinical Sock Work Journal, 15*(1), 43–56.

Mack, I. T. (1974). *Developmental differences in the manifest content of the dreams of normal and disturbed children*. Doctoral Dissertation, Columbia University.

Mahler, M. (1963). Thoughts about development and individuation. *The Psychoanalytical Study of the Child 18*, 307–324.

Mahler, M. (1968). *On human symbiosis and the vicissitudes of individuation*. New York: International Universities Press.

Mahler, M., Pine, F., & Bergman, A. (1975). *The psychological birth of the human infant*. New York: Basil Books.

Markowitz, I. Steadman, Spear, & Symonds. (1963). An investigation of parental recognition of children's dreams. In J. H. Masserman (Ed.), *Violence and War* (pp. 135–151). New York: Grune and Stratton.

Markowitz, I., Bokert, E., Sleser, I., & Taylor, G. (1967). A cybernetil model of dreaming. *Psychiatric Quarterly* (Supplement), *14*, 57–68.

Masserman, J. (1944). Language, behavior, and dynamic psychiatry. *International Journal of Psychoanalysis, 25,* 1–66.

Masterson, J. (1981). *The narcissistic and borderline personalities.* New York: Brunner Mazel.

Masterson, J. F. (1967). *The psychiatric dilemma of adolescence.* Boston: Little, Brown.

Masterson, J. F. (1972). *Treatment of the borderline adolescent: A developmental approach.* New York: Wiley-Interscience.

Meeks, J. E. (1971). *The fragile alliance.* Baltimore: William R. Williams.

Monchaux, C. (1978). Dreaming and the organizing function of the ego. *International Journal of Psychoanalysis, 59,* 443–453.

Offel, D. (1969). *The psychological world of the teenager.* New York: Basic Books.

Offel, D., & Offel, J. B. (1975). *From teenager to young manhood.* New York: Basic Books.

Palombo, S. R. (1978). *Dreaming and memory.* New York: Basil Books.

Piaget, J. (1929). *The child's conception of the world.* New York: Harcourt Brace.

Piaget, J. (1959). *Language and thought of the child.* New York: Humanities Press.

Piaget, J. I. (1962). *Judgement and reasoning in the child.* New York: Humanities Press.

Pivik, T., & Foulkes, D. (1966). Dream deprivation: Effects on dream content. *Science, 153,* 1282–1284.

Rangell, L. (1956). The dream in the practice of psychoanalysis. *Journal of the American Psychoanalytical Association, 4,* 122–137.

Rappaport, D. (1959). A historical survey of psychoanalytical ego psychology. Introduction to Erik Erikson, *Identity and the life cycle.* New York: International Universities Press, p. 547.

Rechtschaffen, A. (1967). Dream reports and dream experiences. *Experimental Neurology,* Supp. 4, 4–15.

Reis, W. (1951). A comparison of the interpretation of dream studies with and without free associations. In M. F. DeMartino (Ed.), *Dreams and Personality Dynamics* (pp. 211–225). Springfield, Ill.: Charles C. Thomas.

Roffwarg, H. Dement, W., Muzio, J., & Fisher, C. (1962). Dream imagery: Relationship to rapid eye movements of sleep. *Archives of general psychiatry, 7,* 235.

Selling, L. S. (1932). Effect of conscious wish upon dream content. *Journal of Abnormal Social Psychology, 27,* 172–178.

Sheppard, E., & Karon, B. (1964). Systematic studies of dreams: Relationship between the manifest dream and associations to the dream elements. *Comp. Psychiatry, 5,* 335–344.

Singer, J. (1966). *Daydreaming.* New York: Random House.

Snyder, F. (1970). The phenomenology of dreaming. In L. Madow & L. H. Snow (Eds.), *The Psychodynamic implications of physiological studies on dreams.* Springfield, Ill.: Charles C. Thomas.

Stern, D. (1985). *The interpersonal world of the infant.* New York: Basic Books.

Trupin, S. (1976). Correlates of ego-level and agency communion in stage REM dreams of 11–13-year-old children. *Journal of Child Psychology and Psychiatry, 17*(3), 169–180.

Van de Castle, R. L. (1971). *The psychology of dreaming.* New York: General Learning Press.

Vaughn, C. J. (1964). Behavior evidence for dreaming in rhesus monkeys. *Physiologist, 7,* 275.

Weisz, R., & Foulkes, D. (1970). Home and laboratory dreams collected under uniform sampling conditions. *Psychophysiology, 6,* 588–596.

White, R. (1974). Strategies of adaptation: An attempt at systematic description. In G., Coello, N., Hamburg, & J. Adams (Eds.), *Coping and adaptation* (pp. 47–68). New York: Basic Books.

Winget, C., & Kramer, M. (1979). *Dimensions of dreams.* Gainsville: University of Florida Press.

Winnicott, D. W. (1965). *The maturational processes and the facilitating environment: Studies in the theory of emotional development.* New York: International Universities Press.

Witty, P. A., & Kopel, W. (1971). The dreams and wishes of elementary school children. *Journal of Educational Psychology, 30,* 199–205.

Index

Ablon, S. L., 8, 23, 26, 36, 38, 63, 107, 113
Adaptive aspects of dreams, 22, 23, 26–27
Adjustment disorders, 129–130, 150
Adler, A., 22
Adolescents, examples of dreams, 147–151
Adolescents and therapy
appeal of dream reports, 112–113, 132–133
dream analysis, 132–135
essential components of therapy, 131
therapeutic relationship, 131
Affective response of dreamer, recall and, 69

Amons and Amons Quick Test, 68, 71
Analysis of variance test, 63, 76
Anderson, J. E., 24, 37
Aserinsky, E., 24, 32
Authority figures in dreams, 181
Autistic phase, 43
Autonomy versus shame and doubt, 149

Beck, H. W., 138
Bergman, 8
Bizarre elements in dreams
emotionally disturbed, 86–87, 94–98
latency-aged child, 144
Blanchard, P., 24, 37
Blanck, G., 42

Blanck, R., 42
Blos, P., 84, 131
Borderline personality, 43
Borkert, E., 23
Bornstein, B., 8
Brenner, C., 20
Bussell, J., 35

Cason, H., 24, 37
Catalano, S., 10
Clinical practice
  adolescents and, 131–135
  improving dream recall, 118–
    119
  as laboratory setting, 110–111
  moderately disturbed and, 138
  recent developments, 7–8
  resistant patient, 138
  school-aged children and, 122–
    130
  severely disturbed and, 136–
    138
  therapist training and use of
    dream content, 119
  young child and, 119–122
Confabulation
  dream research and, 35–37
  reasons for, 192
Consent for study, 61–62, 203–
  204
Cowger, C.D., 90

Defensive aspect of dreams, 21
Dement, W., 35
Development, capacity to dream
  and, 34
Developmental regression, 110
Developmental stages, 8, 173
  changes in dream experience,
    34

dream content and, 23, 26, 44–
  51, 176–177
dream content research, 44–51,
  47
ego pathology and, 43–44
Erikson's stages, 44
Mahler's stages, 42
Developmental stress, 23
Developmental theory, 40–45
  focus of, 40–41
  intrapsychic development, 42–
    43
  major theorists, 42–43, 44
Diagnostic assessment, methods
  of, 9
Divorce and children, examples
  of dreams, 157
Dora, case of, 38
Dream analysis
  adolescents, 132–135
  evaluating risk of, 136–137
  school-aged children, 122–130
  young children, 121–122
Dream content
  adaptive aspects, 22, 23, 26–27
  demystification of, 27
  and developmental stage, 23,
    26, 44–51
  ego functioning and, 22–23,
    107
  of emotionally disturbed, 28–
    29, 47, 48, 86–87, 94–98
  examples of, 12–14
  Freudian view of, 20–22
  improving recall, 118–119
  memory cycle model, 22–23
  new perspective, 107
  significance of, 10–15
  use in treatment, 117–118
Dream journal, 125–126, 191

Dream reports, 8–9, 63
  appeal to adolescents, 112–113, 132–133
  purposes of, 8–9
  sample problem, 32, 36
Dream research, 24–29
  adults, 24
  children, 24–25
  confabulation and, 35–37
  contributions of study to, 105–111
  criticism of, 35–36
  emotionally disturbed children, 28–29, 46–51
  lack of, 31
  longitudinal studies, 106–107
  manifest versus latent content, 37–39
  related to developmental stages, 23, 26
  related to Erikson's stages, 46
  REM-related, 24, 32–33
  suggestions for further study, 111–115
  verbalizing dreams, 25–26
Dream research (present study)
  analytic methods
    qualitative analysis, 82–87, 93–97
    quantitative analysis, 73–82, 87–93
  design/methodology, 57
  hypotheses, 55–56
    testing, 57
  implications of
    clinical practice as laboratory setting, 110–111
    developmental function and dream content, 107–110

dream content of emotionally disturbed, 106–107
  instruments used
    dream rating, 66–67
    Elkan checklist, 65–66
    intelligence test, 68, 71
    socio-economic status measure, 68
    structured recall, 63–65
  interview procedure, 61–62
  population/samples, 57–60
  statistical tests, 62–63, 205–208
  suggestions for further study, 111–115
  summary of study, 97–102
  validity/reliability issues, 68–71
Dreams
  dream cycles, 171–172
  frequency per night, 172, 176
  past interest in, 19–20
  traumatic events and, 177
Dream work, 37–38

Edward, J., 138
Ego defenses, mature defenses, 44
Ego functioning
  dreams and, 22–23, 107
  effects of dream recall, 113–114
Ego and the Mechanisms of Defense, The (Freud), 42
Ego pathology, and developmental phase, 43–44
Ego psychology, 37–38, 44, 112
Elkan, B., 4, 26, 28, 37, 38, 39, 45–46, 49, 55, 65–66, 75–76, 79, 83, 96, 107, 109, 114, 129, 135
Elkan checklist, 63
  basis of, 65

Elkan checklist (*cont.*)
  construction of, 65–66
  instructions to rater, 66–67
  limitations of, 109–111
  response mode, 66
  sample questions, 83–84
  scoring of, 67, 76–79
Emotionally disturbed adoles-
    cents
  degrees of disturbance, 58–59,
    199–200
  developmental level in dream
    content, compared to nor-
    mal group, 73–87
  developmental level reflected
    in dream content, 87–97
  dream content, 86–87, 94–98
  dream content research, 28–29,
    46–51
  severity of disturbance and
    level of dream content,
    90–91, 93–95, 108
Epigenetic principle, 44, 45
Erikson, E., 7, 8, 26, 38–39, 44,
    47, 65, 79
Erikson's stages, 29
  dream content study, 45, 49–
    50
  focus of, 44
  listing of, 197
Expressive ability of dreamer, re-
    call and, 70

Farnsworth, D. L., 131
Fisher, C., 35
Fixation, 8
  stage and pathology, 43–44
Foster, J. C., 24, 37
Foulkes, D., 4, 11, 22, 23, 24–25,

  26, 28, 32, 35, 46–47, 63,
    69, 107, 114
Fraiberg, S., 8, 33
Free association, 20
French, T., 22
Freud, A., 8, 9, 28, 37, 42
Freudian view
  criticism of, 37, 38
  as dominant perspective, 31–
    32
  dream content, 20–22, 24
Freud, S., 8, 19, 21, 31, 37
Fromm, E., 22

Gender differences, nightmares,
    186
Green, M. R., 9, 20, 70, 113
Greenberg, R., 22
Group for the Advancement of
    Psychology, 113

Hall, C., 25, 49
Hartmann, H., 7, 22, 42
Hirschberg, J. C., 22, 25
Hobson, J. A., 32

Identity vs. role confusion, 47,
    83
Infants
  internal distress, 34, 172, 185
  nightmares, 185
  REM sleep, 172
Initiative versus guilt, 13, 135
Interpretation of dreams, effects
    of, 15
Interpretation of Dreams, The
    (Freud), 20, 21
*Introductory Letters of Psychoanaly-
    sis* (Freud), 21
IQ assessment, 68, 71

Jacobson, E., 7, 43
Jersild, A. T., 24, 37
Jersild, L. L., 37
Josselyn, J. M., 131
Jung, C. G., 22
Jungian view of dreams, 22

Karon, B., 39
Kernberg, O., 7, 42, 43
Klein, M., 8, 10, 37
Kleitman, N., 24, 32
Kohut, H., 7, 43
Kopel, W., 24, 37
Kramer, M., 8, 19, 24, 31, 35, 63, 68, 70
Kris, E., 7, 42

Langs, R. J., 29, 48
Larson, J., 23, 46
Latency-aged child
  examples of dreams, 143–146, 180–182; *see also* School-aged children and dream analysis.
Latent content, 23, 195
  dream analysis of school-aged children, 124–125, 128
  versus manifest content in research, 37–39
  nature of, 122
Lewis, M., 8, 33, 42
Lowenstein, 7, 42
Lucente, L., 138

McCarley, R. W., 32
Mack, J. E., 8, 23, 26, 28, 36, 38, 63
Mack, L. T., 4, 48–49, 50, 51, 55, 66, 67, 75, 107, 113, 114

Mahler, M., 8, 42, 43
Manifest content, 23, 26
  versus latent content in research, 37–39
  nature of, 121–122, 194, 195
Markey, F. V., 37
Markowitz, I., 23
Masserman, 34
Masterson, J., 43, 131
Meeks, J. E., 131
Memory cycle model, 22–23
Methodology in studies
  confabulation effects, 33–37
  dream content reports, 8–9, 63
  dream rating, 66–67
  Elkan checklist, 65–66
  manifest versus latent content, 37–39
  structured recall, 63–65
Minnesota Multiphasic Personality Inventory (MMPI), 28
Monchaux, C., 22
Muzio, J., 35

Neurotransmitters, 32–33
Nightmares
  in adults, 186
  age and frequency of, 185–186
  characteristics of, 184
  gender differences, 186
  infancy, 185
  meaning of, 184–185
  reasons for occurrence of, 185–187
Night terrors, characteristics of, 187

Offel, D., 131
One-way analysis of variance, 63

Palombo, S. R., 8, 22
Parents and children's dreams,
    164–167
  communication about dreams,
    193–196
  improving recall, 190–192
Pearlman, C., 22
Pearson correlational coefficient,
    79
Physically ill children, examples
    of dreams, 155–156
Piaget, J., 34, 131, 173
Pine, 8, 42
Pivik, T., 23, 28, 32, 35, 47
Preschoolers, *see also* Young chil-
    dren and therapy
  developmental issues, 178
  examples of dreams, 179–180
Primary process thinking,
    dreams as, 21
Problem solving, 22
Psychoanalytic theory, 10–11

Qualitative analysis
  developmental level and
    dream content, 82–87
  development level reflected in
    dream content, 93–97
Quantitative analysis
  developmental level and
    dream content, emotion-
    ally disturbed vs. normal
    adolescents, 73–82
  development level reflected in
    dream content, emotion-
    ally disturbed adolescents,
    87–93

Radin, M., 46
Rangell, L., 8

Rapid eye movement (REM)
    sleep
  cycles of, 171–172
  dream research, 24, 32–33
  infancy, 33, 172
Rappaport, D., 43
Rardin, 23
Recall
  and affective response of
    dreamer, 69
  artistic expression and, 190–
    191
  and expressive ability of
    dreamer, 70
  improving by parent, 190–192
  improving in clinical practice,
    118–119, 127–128
  methods
    comparison of, 69
    spontaneous recall, 63
    structured recall, 64–65
  and therapeutic relationship,
    113
  validity/reliability issue, 69
Rechtschaffen, A., 28, 35
Recurring dreams, self-identity
    themes, 14–15
Research settings
  clinical practice as, 110–111
  laboratory versus non-labora-
    tory, 63–64
  sleep laboratories, 175–176
Resistant patient, dream content
    analysis and, 138
Roffwarg, H., 35
Russ, W., 39

School-aged children and dream
    analysis, 122–130, 130

dream journal, 125–126
explanation of dreams to child, 122–124
frightening dreams, 128–129
improving dream recall, 127–128
latent content, 124–125, 128
usefulness of, 124
Self-identity themes, recurring dreams, 14–15
Selling, L., 24, 37
Separation-anxiety, 144–145
Separation–individuation phase, 43, 84–85
Severely disturbed adolescents
clinical practice and, 136–138
level of dream content, 90–91, 93–95, 108
Sexual feelings, 180
Sexually abused children, examples of dreams, 153–155
Shepphard, E., 39
Singer, J., 70
Sleep
dreaming cycles, 171–172
stages of, 170–171
Sleser, I., 23
Social issues, 85–86
adolescence, 148
school-aged child, 182
Socio-economic status, 76
measures of, 68, 71
Spear, P., 23
Spontaneous recall
compared to structured recall, 69
criticism of, 63
Steadman, H., 23
Stern, D. 42

Structured recall
compared to spontaneous recall, 69
procedure in, 64–65
Swanson, E., 23, 46
Symbiotic phase, 43
Symonds, J., 23

Taylor, G., 23
Therapeutic relationship, 11, 15, 113
adolescents and, 131
as curative factor, 118–119
Therapy: *see* Clinical practice
Trupin, S., 22
Trust issues, 86
T test, 62, 79, 82

Unconscious, dream content and, 9–10, 20–21, 23–24

Validity and reliability
child-related variables, 70–71
of coded systems for dream content, 70
problems related to, 69
of recall methods, 69
Van de Castle, B. J., 19, 70
Vaughn, C. J., 35

Waking behavior, dreams and, 22
Weisz, R., 32
White, R., 42
Winget, C., 8, 19, 24, 31, 35, 63, 68, 70
Winnicott, D. W., 8
Wish fulfillment, 21, 26, 27
Witty, P. A., 24, 37

Young children and therapy,
     119–122
   clarification of process to child,
     120–121
   dream analysis, 121–122

initial assessment, 119–120
manifest and latent content,
     121–122
methodology, 121
variables and treatment, 120